All Things Anglican

MARCUS THROUP

All Things Anglican

Who We Are and What We Believe

CANTERBURY
PRESS
Norwich

© Marcus Throup 2018

First published in 2018 by the Canterbury Press Norwich
Editorial office
3rd Floor, Invicta House
108–114 Golden Lane
London EC1Y 0TG, UK

www.canterburypress.co.uk

Second impression 2019

Canterbury Press is an imprint of Hymns Ancient & Modern Ltd
(a registered charity)

Ancient
&Modern

Hymns Ancient & Modern® is a registered trademark of Hymns
Ancient & Modern Ltd
13A Hellesdon Park Road, Norwich,
Norfolk NR6 5DR, UK

Scripture quotations are from the New Revised Standard Version of
the Bible, Anglicized Edition, copyright © 1989, 1995 by the Division
of Christian Education of the National Council of the Churches of
Christ in the USA. Used by permission. All rights reserved.

British Library Cataloguing in Publication data

A catalogue record for this book is available
from the British Library

978 1 78622 067 7

Typeset by Regent Typesetting
Printed and bound in Great Britain by
CPI Group (UK) Ltd

Contents

For Luiz and Jessica de Andrade Lima

Preface

One of the privileges of being Diocesan Director of Ordinands (DDO) is that I get to hear inspiring stories of amazing people called by God to serve as leaders in the Church of England. It's fantastically encouraging to see God's Spirit at work, nudging and raising up men and women who are multi-talented and spiritually gifted. We need them! But as I have talked to potential lay ministers, or prepared candidates for the national selection conference for ordained ministry – the Bishops' Advisory Panel (BAP) – I've found that many struggle to grasp certain areas of Anglicanism. Though people who seek out people like me to explore their vocation are Anglicans – some life-long members of the Church of England – many readily admit they are not too hot on topics such as 'sacraments', 'priestly ministry' and 'liturgy'. Usually there is an awareness that the parish down the road does things a bit differently, but the range of alternative approaches can seem confusing. Then again, some candidates are relative newcomers to the Anglican scene and feel unsure or even suspicious about particular things we do or the way we do them. Equally, I have heard the frustration of 'cradle Anglicans' who feel they were never really taught what it means to belong to *this* Church. Many are only vaguely aware of the existence of the worldwide Anglican Communion.

In the face of these challenges, as a theological educator I have done what any teacher would: panicked and reached for the nearest textbooks! Surely an introductory book on Anglicanism would come to my rescue? I found myself revisiting titles I'd read 15 years ago, before my own ordination, and wading through a flood of newer publications. One morning as I sat at my desk a touch frustrated, one of our bishops strolled in. 'What's the problem?' he asked. I explained that I was struggling to find a short textbook on Anglicanism that would cover the essentials in a way that readers would find accessible, practical, informative and engaging.

Don't get me wrong. There are plenty of good books on Anglicanism out there. In fact, there seems to be a minor industry churning out all manner of volumes on Anglican studies, from titanic tomes to pocket-sized paperbacks, from contemporary sound-bites to downloadable classics. On the other hand, as I explained to the bishop, even the 'introductions' tend to assume a level of knowledge and familiarity with terminology that many church members simply don't possess. Increasingly, both at home and overseas, people are coming into the Anglican Church with no prior knowledge or experience of Anglicanism. To such people our Anglican jargon is not only unfamiliar, it can feel alienating, archaic, and even a bit wacky!

Moreover, things are changing so fast in the Anglican world that some good works from just a few years ago are rapidly becoming outdated. Our blessed acronyms seem to be multiplying like rabbits, and key topics from a few years back are already yesterday's news. Another issue is style: authors often approach Anglicanism from a cerebral historical perspective which isn't to everyone's taste. Similarly, the erudite academic style of many books suits some but can be off-putting for others. 'Well, you'll just have to write something yourself!' said the bishop. This, then, is my attempt at *writing something myself*.

I want to be upfront from the start, and admit that while I've taught Anglicanism overseas and in the UK, I can't claim to be an expert. On the plus side this means that I'm unlikely to bog readers down with complexities and detail, and I've tried not to overdo footnotes. They appear usually in conversation with something in the literature on Anglicanism. Of course, some readers might want to go deeper than I feel able to go here, and the Bibliography should signpost some useful titles.

Hopefully, everyone will get *something* out of this book. Since many people move to the Anglican Church from other Christian Churches, it will be of particular use to this group. It will be instructive for Anglicans who want to learn more about their Church, and it will be of interest to adults preparing for baptism or confirmation in the Church of England and other Anglican or Episcopal (they're all part of the family) Churches. It will help inform those who are giving serious thought to going forward for some form of Anglican ministry, be it lay or ordained. It may also give people from other churches or faith traditions a window on what Anglicanism is about and where it might be headed. Above all, it begins with the concrete reality and richness that is the worldwide Anglican Communion rather than tacking this on at the end as a curious but unavoidable aside. Part 2 includes some essential sources on which Anglican identity and theology are founded, grouping these together for reference purposes.

On a different note, I hope that more experienced Anglican writers might excuse my *un-Anglican* approach: where I've spotted 'elephants in the room' I've chosen to go over and chat to them rather than pretend they're not there. As will become clear, I base my account on over 20 years of personal experience of Anglican mission and ministry as well as book-based research. Other people will see things from other perspectives, but I have tried to be fair-handed and include a broad spectrum of views and opinions. That, at least, is a truly *Anglican* approach.

My thanks go to a number of people – to Bishop David Williams, for giving me the initial encouragement I needed to get writing, and to the Revd Christine Smith for encouraging me to submit the script to Canterbury Press. To William Cole from Winchester Cathedral's Resource Room, for keeping me well stocked with all manner of books on Anglicanism. To Bishop Tim Dakin and my colleague the Revd Paul Dunthorne for reading and commenting on the script. Similarly, to the Revd Dr Andrew Angel, the Revd Luiz Lima, and my sister Jessica Lima. By way of clarification, the views expressed in this book are not theirs, nor are they in any way responsible for any inaccuracies or errors.

PART I

Questions and Answers

I

What do we mean by 'Anglicanism'?

The *Oxford English Dictionary* defines 'Anglicanism' as 'the faith and practices of the Anglican Christian Churches'.[1] What the dictionary doesn't tell us is that there are something in the region of 85 million Anglicans dotted around the planet whose 'practices' and understanding of 'the faith' vary considerably. In reality, 'Anglicanism' is a slippery word, difficult to pin down in so far as it means different things to different people.[2] It doesn't help that there has been disagreement among leading Anglican thinkers as to whether the very term 'Anglicanism' should be used at all.[3] Throw in contemporary hot-potatoes such as the Church and sexuality – where opposing voices claim to be *the true voice* of Anglicanism – and we begin to get a feel for just how confusing all things Anglican can be.

How, then, do we even begin to talk about Anglicanism? Where should we start? One possibility would be to dip into the troubled

---

1 https://en.oxforddictionaries.com/definition/anglicanism, accessed 4 July 2017.

2 Some Anglican thinkers prefer to speak of the 'Anglican Way' and are suspicious of the term 'Anglicanism', as it might seem to suggest a kind of ideology when really it concerns a way of life and faith. See, for example, Terry M. Brown, 'Anglican Way or Ways?' (pp. 620–35), in Mark D. Chapman, Sathianathan Clarke and Martyn Percy (eds), *The Oxford Handbook of Anglican Studies*, Oxford: Oxford University Press, 2016, p. 621.

3 Cf. Colin Podmore, *Aspects of Anglican Identity*, London: Church House Publishing, 2005, pp. 38–41, citing (1) John Macquarrie and Michael Ramsey as those who have questioned the appropriateness of the term 'Anglicanism' on the disputed grounds that the Anglican Churches have no set confession or unique belief system, and (2) Stephen Sykes and Paul Avis who defend the use of the term, believing there to be something identifiably distinctive about the Anglican way of living the Christian faith.

waters of history, working forwards from King Henry VIII and his sixteenth-century version of Brexit. It was Henry's Act of Supremacy (1534) that gave the English Church its independence from Rome, paving the way for what came to be known as the Church of England. So, we could begin our Anglican studies in the 1500s, but that would inevitably narrow our focus on England when there is so much more to Anglicanism than the Church of England.

Instead of getting bogged down with history, a more cutting-edge approach might be via the Christian blogosphere and social media. If we want to get a grip on Anglicanism today, surely we just whip out our smartphones and listen in on the latest internet conversations about Anglican identity? Maybe, but those virtual arenas are not always forums for healthy and fair exchanges. For every helpful webpage there are half a dozen others filled with 'fake news' and the grumblings of axe-grinding pundits. What, then, should be our approach?

To try and get a balance, we'll gauge where we are today while keeping an eye on our roots, tracking the ways in which the past has shaped our Anglican present. Rather than charging into current debates where 'conservative' and 'liberal' theologians square up to one another, we'll begin not with the experts, nor with complicated ideas, but with the ordinary *extraordinary* Christian men, women and children in the Church itself.

By this I'm not pretending we can sidestep hard questions or give contentious issues the slip, but I *am* suggesting that any conversation about Anglicanism needs to begin and end with Anglican *people* – their voices need to be heard and their views need to be respected. When we're thrashing out our theology we need to be careful that it's our ideas and ideals we're thrashing. Beating people around the head with a Bible is unlikely to solve our problems in a hurry.

Let's begin, then, with Anglican *people* in the twenty-first century. Who are they? First, Anglicans are Christians who belong within the One Church of Christ which is both catholic, i.e. universal, and apostolic, i.e. it traces its *spiritual* DNA to the apostles, and ultimately to Jesus himself. Its historical roots are British and can be traced to the late period of the Roman Empire when Christianity travelled west.[4] A monumental turning point was Henry VIII's spat with the Pope and his exit from Europe's Roman Catholic landmass. In more recent times, though, the Anglican Church has grown outwards from its English centre, forming an interconnected international entity with impressive reach and flexibility.

The Anglican Church is a family present in 165 countries, whose members number millions upon millions of people. What this underlines is that, today, Anglicanism is a truly global and richly diverse expression of the Christian Church. To really appreciate just what this means, we might draw a mental picture of our average Anglican churchgoer. Who comes to mind, I wonder? For those of us living in the UK, Europe, North America or Australasia, it might come as a bit of a wake-up call to learn that the average Anglican today is a young, poor, black woman living in sub-Saharan Africa.[5] Let's picture her for a second: she expresses her faith in indigenous songs of praise, and her outlook on life is framed by hope in Jesus. It's very likely that she is a member of the Mothers' Union – a movement that began in a sleepy English village, but today is a vibrant force all over Africa. While she has one eye on heaven above, her lively spirituality is grounded in a day-to-day routine of early rising and hard work, a routine that ensures the survival of her young family.

This snapshot of our average twenty-first-century Anglican points to an arresting reality: geographically, numerically and culturally

---

4 We're not sure who first brought the gospel to the British Isles or when exactly. While legend has it that Joseph of Arimathea brought the message of Jesus to Britain this is not normally given much credence. The likelihood is that Christianity arrived in Britain with eastern traders and possibly converts from the Roman military ranks. This would almost certainly have taken place 100–200 years after Jesus' death and resurrection, but may well have occurred earlier than that.

5 Cf. Philip Jenkins, *The Next Christendom: The Coming of Global Christianity*, Oxford: Oxford University Press, 2002.

the centre of gravity of the Anglican Church has shifted from the northern to the southern hemisphere. For those who are fond of statistics, researchers estimate that in 1972, 62% of all Anglicans were based in Europe and that by 2010 this figure had halved to 31%. Conversely, in 1972, African Anglicans made up 16% of all Anglicans worldwide, but this had increased to 58% in 2010.[6]

It is in the so-called Global South – which is Africa, South East Asia and Latin America – where Christianity is growing at a phenomenal rate. Whereas the UK has become a case study in 'dechristianization', with the Church of England and other denominations battling declining membership, it is estimated that there are now over 20 million Anglicans in Nigeria alone.[7] A Nigerian bishop is rumoured to have commented that church planting is occurring at such a rate in his country that people have been known to say, 'Bishop, please come to our region: you're not aware of this, but we've just planted two hundred churches and we're ready to become a new diocese!'

That impressive growth pattern isn't restricted to English-speaking countries and former British colonies. Before the early 1970s there was virtually no Anglican presence in the Democratic Republic of Congo, but in 2015 the Congolese Anglicans could boast over 500 clergy and a membership of 237,000.[8] Next door in the

---

6 Todd M. Johnson and Gina A. Zurlo, 'The Changing Demographics of Global Anglicanism, 1970–2010' (pp. 37–53), p. 37, in David Goodhew (ed.), *Growth and Decline in the Anglican Communion: 1980 to the Present*, London: Routledge, 2017.

7 For a carefully nuanced view of the 'narrative decline' of Christianity and the Church of England, see Nick Spencer, *Doing Good: A Future for Christianity in the 21st Century*, London: Theos, 2017, pp. 15–29, and David Heywood, *Reimagining Ministry*, London: SPCK, 2011, pp. 15–16. For the classic study on the Church in the UK as a model of 'dechristianization' in contrast to the growth in the Global South, see Philip Jenkins, *The Next Christendom: The Coming of Global Christianity*, Oxford: Oxford University Press, 2002. For a different view on the gloomy figures around the decline of Church of England attendance, see Martyn Percy, *Anglicanism: Confidence, Commitment and Communion*, Farnham: Ashgate, 2013, pp. 75–88.

8 David Goodhew (ed.), *Growth and Decline in the Anglican Communion: 1980 to the Present*, London: Routledge, 2017, p. 10.

former Portuguese colony of Angola, there are around 100,000 Anglicans – not bad considering the devastating civil war that raged there from 1975 to 2002.[9]

The change in Anglican demographics with this massive shift to the southern hemisphere coincides with what Andrew Walls calls 'the Great Reverse Migration' – that is, the mass movement of mainly African and Asian people to Europe and North America.[10] One important implication of this is that whereas the Church of England has long been a missional, sending Church, it must again learn to *receive*. The same could be said of the English-speaking Anglican/Episcopal Churches in the USA, Canada, Australia and New Zealand. So just as missionaries from the East brought the gospel of Jesus Christ to the British Isles in the first couple of centuries CE, two thousand years on, African, Asian and Latino Christians are arriving in the 'mission field' that is the so-called developed West.

From the perspective of western churches some might view this missional shift as a kind of role-reversal, but God calls people when he likes, from where he likes, and however he likes. More positively than 'role-reversal' the current trend should be about the positive recognition – explicit in Anglican mission societies such as Church Mission Society (CMS) – that mission must be *from anywhere to everywhere*. To its credit, the Church of England now recognizes and values the contribution that immigrants and migrant Christian communities are making to life in the UK. One of its immediate aims is to increase the number of BAME (Black, Asian, Minority Ethnic) leaders, and the more successful it is in realizing this objective, the more spiritually enriched our English churches will become.

---

9 The 100,000 statistic was supplied by the Diocesan Secretary (personal communication) on a visit I made to the Diocese of Angola in August 2017.

10 Andrew Walls 'Afterword: Christian Mission in a 500 Year Context', p. 194 in Cathy Ross and Andrew Walls, *Mission in the 21st Century: Exploring the Five Marks of Global Mission*. Maryknoll, NY: Orbis, 2008.

Globally, the multi-ethnic, multi-lingual family of Anglicans is known as the Anglican Communion – essentially, a worldwide *community*. The basic building blocks of the Communion are the 'Provinces' which, for convenience, may be thought of as geographical areas, but are really about *peoples* rather than places. In total there are 39 Provinces, though the Church of England consists of just two – the historic 'Sees' of Canterbury and York. The Scottish Episcopal Church and the Church in Wales have historical links with the Church of England, but they are independent Provinces, as is the Church of Ireland.

In some world regions a Province might be made up of multiple nations or territories – for example, the Church of the Province of the Southern Cone, encompassing several South American countries; the Church of the Province of South East Asia, covering Singapore and West Malaysia; the Anglican Church in Aotearoa, New Zealand and Polynesia, and the Church of the Province of Central Africa, covering Botswana, Malawi, Zambia and Zimbabwe.[11] Such arrangements mean that the ethnic make-up of several Provinces is massively diverse, and this is something that brings richness and challenges – be these logistical, cultural and/or theological.

In the Anglican world, Provinces are broken down into smaller geographical units called dioceses. These in turn are made up of parishes, and sometimes 'mission plants' or similar terminology. Just as each Province or large region is overseen by an archbishop, each diocese is overseen by a diocesan bishop, and every parish is overseen by a parish priest or other clergy leader. New mission plants are sometimes pioneered by clergy, but more often the initiative and day-to-day running is in the hands of lay leaders. Whereas mission strategies in the past have some-

---

11 For a comprehensive list of the member Churches of the Anglican Communion, see www.anglicancommunion.org.

times depended too much on clergy input and presence, creating an unhealthy 'paternalistic' model that stands or falls with one influential individual, more recently 'every-member ministry' has proven effective overseas. For example, the Anglican Church in Mozambique makes effective use of *catechists* (teachers who talk people through, and provide instruction on, the basics of the faith) to disciple people and sow the seeds of new churches. In Latin America, fledgling mission plants often begin in people's homes.

Within the Anglican Communion there is an impressive ethnic and cultural diversity which is to be celebrated and cherished. One friend of mine visited the Diocese of the Arctic and the Inuit people, and a former student is a regular visitor to the Anglican Church of the indigenous tribes of Papua New Guinea. My diocesan bishop worked with the Anglican Church in Kenya, my team leader led the Anglican Church in Amsterdam, and for 15 years I served in the Anglican Church in Brazil. Geographically we might be poles apart, but as Anglicans we belong to the same branch of the Christian family.

There is, then, great diversity – culturally and ethnically – there are also significant differences in approach to contemporary issues and the ways in which we 'do church'. As in all families, there are genuine differences of opinion and at times we may fall out with one another. In recent decades this has been painfully true in relation to the ordination of women priests and the con-secration of women bishops, as well as in regard to debates on human sexuality. Twenty-first-century Anglicanism is fighting hard to preserve its *unity*, endeavouring to hold together different groups of people who have the same Anglican DNA but radically different perspectives on some key topics.

The very notion of a *unity* that makes room for and celebrates *diversity* is a key principle of Anglicanism. Related to this is the concept of *comprehensiveness*, which has been defined as 'agree-ment on fundamentals, while tolerating disagreement on matters on which Christians may differ without feeling the necessity of breaking communion'.[12] Thus, the principle of comprehensiveness implies an openness to different perspectives and interpretations and the recognition that ongoing dialogue can gradually help us discover God's truth more fully.

On this definition of *comprehensiveness*, though, where do we draw the line between the 'fundamentals' and 'matters on which Christians may differ'?[13] How do we know which is which and who gets to decide? As diverse individuals and people groups from every corner and crevice of the planet, on *what* do we base our unity? These are all important questions and Anglicanism is still working out its answers to some of them. Nevertheless, there are some basic principles concerning unity that we can identify and agree on, as we shall see.

Basic principles of unity

First, we are united as brothers and sisters in Jesus Christ, mindful of the foundational scriptural teaching on unity:

> [bear] with one another in love, making every effort to maintain the unity of the Spirit in the bond of peace. There is one body and one Spirit, just as you were called to the one hope of your calling, one Lord, one faith, one baptism, one God and Father of all, who is above all and through all and in all. (Ephesians 4.2–6)

As Anglicans, our common Christian belief is expressed not in any specifically *Anglican* statement but in biblical truths. The truths I have in mind are those summed up in the historic creeds

---

12 This definition was used at the 1968 Lambeth Conference.

13 A similar critique was made by S. W. Sykes in *The Integrity of Anglicanism*, London: Mowbray, 1978, and endorsed more recently by George Lings in 'Chapter 9¾: Can the Idea of a Reproductive Strand in Church Identity Fit with Church of England Ecclesiology?' (see the Church Army website: www. churcharmy.org/Groups/287912/Church_Army/Church_Army/Our_work/ Research/Reproducing_Churches/Reproducing_Churches.aspx).

– that is, the Apostles' Creed and the Nicene Creed contained in Part 2 of this book.[14] The creeds affirm belief in God as Father, Son and Holy Spirit and focus attention on Jesus' death and resurrection as historical events with eternal significance. They also express belief in the Church as the people of God down the ages. The 'communion of saints' are all those who are restored to relationship with the Father through Christ's death and resurrection which bring us unending life (cf. John 11.25–26).

It's amazing to think that every Sunday the creeds' ancient statements of faith are publicly affirmed throughout our Anglican Churches by millions of people in hundreds of different languages. What is more, the public profession of our core beliefs connects us not just with the present generation, but with those who went before us in the faith. Thus there is continuity with what is sometimes known as the 'Church triumphant' as well as with the 'Church militant', where 'militant' signifies the Christians who are presently alive and 'fighting the good fight'.

Our baptism and our creedal identity bring us together as Anglicans, but also unite us with Christians from other traditions. Whether Roman Catholic or Pentecostal, all those baptized in the name of the Holy Trinity and who sign up to these truths are, as it were, our 'extended' family in Christ. The recognition that Anglicans are part of the one true catholic (that is, universal) Church that is founded on Jesus Christ was particularly emphasized by theologians such as Richard Hooker (1554–1600) and Archbishop of Armagh James Ussher (1581–1656).[15] We still emphasize this today and it helps us remember that Anglicanism can never be the 'be all and end all'. The Church is much bigger

---

14 It is apt, therefore, that in David Edwards's book *What Anglicans Believe in the Twenty-first Century*, London: Continuum, 2002, the first chapters are titled respectively 'We believe in the Father'; 'We believe in the Son' and 'We believe in the Holy Spirit', illustrating the inherently creedal and Trinitarian pattern of Anglican belief.

15 See Paul Avis, *Anglicanism and the Christian Church*, London, T&T Clark, 2002, pp. 69–71.

than we are, and Christ – *not* our Church – is to be the object of our worship and our number one priority.

Beyond our core Christian identity that we share with fellow believers from many other Christian Churches, we are further united as *Anglicans* in a common way of 'being Church'. Regardless of the language we speak and the corner of the globe we inhabit, Anglican life and worship will place a dual emphasis on the importance of God's word and the importance of the sacraments instituted by Christ himself – that is, Holy Baptism and Holy Communion.

Whatever else 'Anglican identity' or the 'Anglican way' might be said to include, at its very core is the pairing of 'word' and 'sacrament'. As mentioned above, this special focus is derived from Jesus' life and teaching as recorded in the New Testament. It is fair to say, though, that the twin 'word'/'sacrament' emphasis was renewed, and in some ways restored, in the theology that was hammered out from the time of the Reformation. It is a feature of the 'historic formularies' that have underpinned Anglican identity for centuries. The 'historic formularies' are: the 39 Articles of Religion; the Book of Common Prayer (BCP); and the Ordinal – that is, the ordering/ordaining of bishops, priests and deacons.

The 39 Articles comprise a series of statements drawn up in the Church of England at the time of the Reformation. While some Articles are more relevant than others – a fair few are bound up with essentially medieval issues – they remain part of our genetic make-up as Anglicans. The Articles affirm word and sacrament separately, but the dual emphasis appears in Article 19, which states that the Church exists where the Bible is preached and the sacraments are properly administered:

> The visible Church of Christ is a congregation of faithful men, in which the pure Word of God is preached, and the Sacraments be duly ministered.

What is explicit in the Articles is implicit throughout the Book of Common Prayer and its more modern versions such as the Common Worship series, and the majority of similar books drawn up in other Provinces of the Anglican Communion. Bible readings and scriptural sentences undergird every twist and turn of our Anglican liturgy. While the liturgy in its entirety has a sacramental flavour, the orders of service for the sacraments are held to be of especial importance. In the majority of global Anglican Churches, Holy Communion is still the 'main event' in terms of weekly services.

Again, the Ordinal – or service of ordination for deacons, priests and bishops – underlines Anglicanism's twin focus of 'word' and 'sacrament'. This is neatly summed up in the words of the Preface of the contemporary Common Worship service:

> The Church of England is part of the One, Holy, Catholic and Apostolic Church, worshipping the one true God, Father, Son and Holy Spirit. It professes the faith uniquely revealed in the Holy Scriptures and set forth in the catholic creeds, which faith the Church is called upon to proclaim afresh in each generation. Led by the Holy Spirit, it has borne witness to Christian truth in its historic formularies, the Thirty-nine Articles of Religion, the Book of Common Prayer, and the Ordering of Bishops, Priests, and Deacons.[16]

What is said here of 'The Church of England' is true also of the Anglican Churches that make up the Anglican Communion. In their own services of ordination or licensing of clergy similar statements are made. Equally, the 'Declaration of Assent' made by the person being ordained or licensed is similar in many Anglican Churches. It too stresses the word/sacrament pairing:

---

16 These words feature in the Preface to the 'Declaration of Assent' in the liturgy of the Church of England and closely parallel Canon A5 of the Church of England. In relation to the discussion above, note how the Church of England situates itself within the 'One, Holy, Catholic and Apostolic Church'.

I (Name) do so affirm, and accordingly declare my belief in the faith which is revealed in the Holy Scriptures and set forth in the catholic creeds and to which the historic formularies of the Church of England bear witness; and in public prayer and administration of the sacraments, I will use only the forms of service which are authorized or allowed by Canon.[17]

Moving from these landmark documents to contemporary church life, to an extent we share a common Anglican way of worship and prayer. Whereas the specifics can and do differ, it's safe to say that the broad contours of our church services are pretty much the same the world over. This is because the Anglican liturgy formulated in the sixteenth century at the time of the English Reformation has become the backbone of the prayer books in the Provinces of the Anglican Communion.

A few years ago I was serving on a clergy team in an Anglican cathedral in Brazil. After taking a Sunday morning service, I greeted an English visitor at the door who remarked: 'I don't speak Portuguese so I didn't understand a word of the service but I knew exactly what was going on in each part of it!' That's because the *shape* of our liturgy is identifiably Anglican. In other words, the pattern of our prayer and the way we worship is broadly universal. A service with a welcome, a time of confession, Scripture reading, reflection/sermon, Holy Communion, blessing and sending out into the wider world is common to the vast majority of Anglican Churches from Australia to Zambia.

On the other hand, it would be misleading to suggest that the *style* of worship or prayer is replicated the world over. The sung 'Mass' I experienced recently in Luanda in Angola sounds radically different from our English choral traditions. Again, a service in Chile would have a very different feel from a service in Uruguay, and what one might experience in South Africa is likely to be quite different from Anglican worship in Uganda.

17 For the history and development of the 'Declaration of Assent', see Colin Podmore, *Aspects of Anglican Identity*, London: Church House Publishing, 2005, pp. 43–57.

As a general rule, Anglicanism welcomes such local contextual-ization and variation, provided that the essential biblical, creedal and doctrinal foundations remain in place.

We have seen how Anglicans are united as followers of Jesus Christ and as members of the catholic and apostolic Church. A desire to hold together word and sacrament is a defining characteristic of our common Anglican identity, an identity rooted in history and tradition in so far as it is anchored in the historic formularies that have been passed down from one generation to the next. All around the globe, the Provinces of the Anglican Communion provide a way of worshipping God that is identifiably Anglican while building in their unique cultural emphases.[18] The unity and diversity that we experience in the worldwide Anglican Com-munion is a tremendous blessing, something to thank God for and something worth fighting for.

Readers of this book who have been part of the Anglican Church for a while and who have followed developments on the inter-national stage might think that this vision of the Anglican Communion is over-optimistic or perhaps out of touch. Isn't the Anglican Communion increasingly *divided* rather than united? Isn't it true that there is more disunity than unity, more discord than harmony? Perhaps, partly, but when I say that the Com-munion is 'something worth fighting for' I speak as someone who has experienced that painful tug of war first-hand. Those who know just how precious our Anglican family is will challenge anything that damages – or threatens to damage – our essential unity in Christ.

That's not to say that there is zero room for change and adap-tation within Anglicanism. Historically, the development of both the Church of England and worldwide Anglican Churches has been about negotiating changing circumstances in a changing world through prayerful reflection and collaborative thinking.

18 We will look at the Anglican Communion more closely in Chapter 8 – particularly its so-called 'instruments of unity', which are further foci for unity and our common Anglican identity.

To borrow St Paul's language, as Anglicans there is a sense in which we are constantly 'working out our faith with fear and trembling' (Philippians 2.12) as we engage with society and pray for our leaders, both religious and secular. Nevertheless, anything that is divisive or potentially divisive sits uneasily with the biblical principle we quoted above: 'make every effort to keep unity in the bond of the Spirit' (Ephesians 4.3). Why? Because we are talking not merely about ideals and ideas, but about *people*. God's people.

So, remind me, what do we mean by 'Anglicanism'?

This chapter has approached the question 'What is Anglicanism?' by posing a *who* question, a *where* question and a *what* question – who are Anglicans, where are they located, and what do they believe? In answering these questions we have introduced the Anglican Communion and this will be taken up more fully in Chapter 8. We have also begun to touch on some principles and writings that are integral to Anglican theology, something we will explore further in Chapter 4.

If we were to tie our Anglican identity down, we might loosely define the Anglican Church as a multi-million-member branch of Christianity present all over the world, but with historical roots in Great Britain and England (*Angle* = like Anglo-Saxon). We have found that Anglicans around the world have several foundational things in common, such as an inherent valuing of both 'word' and 'sacrament', and a unity built around the statement of our Christian faith as set out in the historic creeds.

The 'historic formularies' – the 39 Articles of Religion, the Book of Common Prayer and the Ordinal – are our common legacy. While Anglicanism allows for much diversity in all sorts of ways, it strives to preserve *unity* in diversity. We have seen that Anglicanism has been shaped by events of history that took place long ago in Europe, and especially in England, but recognize that today it is a dynamic, worldwide expression of the Christian faith.

Questions for individual or group reflection

1 What was the most surprising thing that this chapter has highlighted for you?
2 To what extent would it be true to claim that Anglicanism started with King Henry VIII?
3 How true is the claim that 'Anglicans don't have any doctrine or basic statement of belief'?
4 Does the fact that Anglicanism places value on the early Christian creeds and honours the 'historic formularies' mean that it is old-fashioned and unable to adapt to a changing world?
5 Can you think of your own definition of 'Anglicanism' in the light of what this chapter has discussed?

2

Why does the parish down the road do things differently?

In Norwich, if you stand in just the right place on a particular street, it's possible to view several different churches within a stone's throw of one another. They are all Anglican churches, but just because they are close geographically doesn't mean they are all the same. One of the things that can puzzle visitors to different Anglican churches is the great variety of service and worship styles found in them.

At St Mary's a robed choir files through the ancient building in procession, led by someone, called the crucifer, carrying an ornate cross. The service, called 'Mass', is led by a richly attired priest, possibly assisted by a deacon and acolytes (people who assist the priest) bearing candles, whose chanting of the words of the service prompts sung responses from the congregation. Just down the road at St Chad's, there's a different kind of singing as scores of young people jump up and down to the ear-splitting sound of drums and electric guitars. The vicar, dressed in everyday clothes, stands at a podium on the stage, projecting images from his iPad as he preaches.

'St Mary's' and 'St Chad's' are fictional, but the scenes described above are true to life. The newcomer to the Anglican Church is often left puzzling why it is that the parish down the road does things so differently. Why do St Mary's use something called the Book of Common Prayer, singing words that date back to 1662, when St Chad's has huge screens displaying contemporary pictures and informal modern prayers? Why is it that at St Mary's they have 'Mass' every Sunday, and even during the week, when at St Chad's they *do* '[Holy] Communion' just once a month? Why is St Chad's so chilled with such a contemporary feel, when St Mary's is so traditional and the epitome of formality?

Throwing in a few more fictional churches and their true-to-life scenarios, why is it that St Martin's 'won't have a woman vicar' when Revd Sheila down at St Matthew's is loved to bits by her congregation? Why do the folks at St Leonard's call Bob the vicar 'Father Bob' and why on earth does he lead services with his back to everybody? Why does Revd Kev at St Mark's preach for 30 minutes when Revd Ted at St Bede's says all he wants to say in five minutes? Why does Revd Sarah of St Saviour's use incense when Revd Pauline at St Peter's isn't keen on candles?

Before giving specific answers to these and other 'why?' questions, I want to try and explain in general terms why the Anglican Church is so diverse or *broad,* as theologians tend to describe it. To find the answer we need to go back in time to the Reformation in Europe. Some 500 years ago Martin Luther nailed his 95 theses to the door of Wittenberg Cathedral. This was the start of the Reformation – where groups within the Roman Catholic Church protested against certain practices and teachings and ended up breaking away from it. The shock waves were felt around the continent. And when Henry VIII broke with the Roman Catholic Church – for both personal and political reasons – declaring himself Head of the English Church, the way was opened for change and reform in the Church of England.

Influenced first by Martin Luther and later by the Swiss Reformer John Calvin, the Archbishop of Canterbury, Thomas Cranmer, wrote 12 homilies or mini sermons to teach the doctrine of 'justification by faith alone' and to stress the importance of reading the Bible in parish churches. While certain statements he made in what would eventually become the 39 Articles oppose particular aspects of Roman Catholic teaching – the interpretation of Holy Communion as 'transubstantiation' (the belief that the bread is literally transformed into Jesus' body and the wine into his blood in Holy Communion) – Cranmer was not about to throw out the baby with the bath water. Just as the apostle Paul had taught 'test everything, hold on to that which is good' (1 Thessalonians 5.21), when Cranmer wrote the English liturgy – that is, the services of worship and prayers – he retained elements from the Benedictine tradition and blended these with Reformation principles and teachings.[1] As Professor Rudolph Heinze explains:

> In January 1549 Parliament approved the first English prayer book and ordered its use throughout the kingdom. It replaced a confusing melange of books that had been used in the English church and drew on the best liturgical traditions of the past as well as more modern Catholic and Protestant reform liturgies. While leaving no doubt on the essential doctrines of the Reformation, Archbishop Cranmer showed great moderation in balancing traditional and Reformed rites.[2]

It emerges, then, that at its very historical core the Church of England welded together two traditions, the Catholic and the Reformed. This was, and is still, widely regarded as the genius of Anglicanism: it is a 'broad church', capable of embracing both traditions and this remains central to its identity today. From the sixteenth century onwards, with the rise and fall of different monarchs and bishops, the Church would swing either towards the Catholic or the Reformed end of the spectrum. Sometimes a complete reversal was sought. Thus, Queen Mary I, Henry VIII's elder daughter who reigned from 1553 to 1558, is remembered as a staunch Roman Catholic determined to reverse all the changes made in the Reformation so as to restore Catholicism

---

1 Cf. Kenneth Stevenson, 'Anglican Aesthetics' (pp. 165–75), in Mark D. Chapman, Sathianathan Clarke and Martyn Percy (eds), *The Oxford Handbook of Anglican Studies*, Oxford: Oxford University Press, 2016, p. 169, on how the 'Collect for Purity' originates in the priest's preparation before Mass in the *Sarum rite* (the order of services used in the Church of England from the eleventh century) and how the 'Prayer of Humble Access' goes back to Anselm (Archbishop of Canterbury 1093–1109).

2 Rudolph W. Heinze, *Reform and Conflict: From the Medieval World to the Wars of Religion AD 1350–1648, Volume Four*, Oxford: Monarch Books, 2006, p. 215.

to the British Isles. Famously, Mary's violent persecution of the Protestant Reformers earned her the nickname 'bloody Mary'.[3] However, her half-sister Elizabeth I was a Protestant monarch, broadly concerned to steer a conciliatory middle line between the two traditions – while retaining her position as 'Supreme Governor' of the Church of England. This title was conferred on Elizabeth in the Act of Supremacy, one of two Acts of Parliament that formed the 'Elizabethan Religious Settlement'. This meant the Church of England would officially become, at least in principle, the Church for all throughout the land, presided over, ultimately, by the reigning monarch. The second Act was the Act of Uniformity, which had the effect of *regulating* and *authorizing* Cranmer's second 1552 prayer book, but with some key changes.

Famously, the authorized prayer book – which at one level sought to legitimate a Reformed perspective – also preserved (albeit in tweaked form) the Eucharistic liturgy and the rules concerning priestly vestments in order to retain its Catholic roots. In the words of the 'distribution' – that is, when the bread and wine are offered to the 'communicant' (the person taking Holy Communion) – the 1552 book had championed the more Protestant/Reformed tradition by stressing the 'memorial' aspect of the Eucharist with the following words that are still in use today:

> Take and eat this in remembrance that Christ died for thee and feed on him in thy heart with thanksgiving; drink this in remembrance that Christ's blood was shed for thee and be thankful.

The emphasis here on a Reformed 'memorial' interpretation of Jesus' sacrifice on the cross was now counterbalanced with additional sentences plucked from the 1549 prayer book which, without necessarily implying transubstantiation, had a more Catholic ring to them.[4] These words still feature in Anglican Eucharistic services today:

---

3 In what was a turbulent and violent period for the Church, it should also be remembered that there were Catholic martyrs of the English Reformation.
4 With time, the Church of England developed its understanding of

The body of our Lord Jesus Christ which was given for thee, preserve thy body and soul unto everlasting life; the blood of our Lord Jesus Christ which was shed for thee, preserve thy body and soul unto everlasting life.

While the annals of history tell the tragic tale of bitter conflicts between Catholics and Protestants, Anglican worship and theology at its best holds together key ingredients of the Catholic and Reformed approaches and is willing to draw on the riches of each tradition. In places, such as in our example concerning Holy Communion, there is a creative tension between the traditions – and perhaps even an attractive synthesis. Anglicanism is often referred to as a *via media* – a middle way – between Roman Catholicism and Protestantism and maybe it is. We can be thankful that we have such a rich heritage of worship upon which to draw.

Those in the middle, though, are always likely to come under fire from more radical groups on the outer edges of the religious spectrum, and this has been the case in England from the reign of Elizabeth I to that of Elizabeth II. It is also an issue in the wider Anglican Communion, not least in majority Roman Catholic countries. In Latin America, for example, Anglicans can be regarded with suspicion by Catholics as 'fake Catholics', and by Protestants as weird hybrids who seem far too Catholic to be genuine 'evangelicos' – that is, Protestant Christians.[5]

Eucharistic theology in dialogue with Luther and Calvin and ruminated on the 'doctrine of real presence' as the best way to understand the sacrament. This doctrine teaches that in the power of the Holy Spirit, Christ becomes present to his people through the sacrament – this is a mystery that defies rational explanation.

5 I am grateful to my colleague Paul Dunthorne who points out that this was exactly the problem Anglican theologian Richard Hooker (1554–1600) faced in England many centuries ago. As Dunthorne puts it, 'Against the Roman Catholics, Hooker stressed the biblical nature of the Church of England based on Word and Sacrament. Against the Puritans, who saw the Church of England as only half-reformed, Hooker emphasized the value of tradition and reason in the interpretation and application of Scripture.'

Back to St Mary's, St Chad's and the 'parish down the road' ...

Clearly the different emphases in the Catholic and Reformed traditions of the sixteenth century are a million miles away from the differences we mentioned previously between St Mary's and St Chad's, or are they? History teaches us that to a large degree Anglicanism has been open to different influences and multiple interpretations. Over the centuries, it has incorporated and allowed for diverse perspectives and various ways of worshipping God. Our 'official' liturgy seeks to include believers of all persuasions and is designed to be used by all. That's why we use the word 'common' – for example, the Book of *Common* Prayer, and in the contemporary liturgy of the Church of England, *Common* Worship. When theologians speak about the 'inclusiveness' or 'comprehensiveness' of Anglicanism, the historical and theological backstory is this concern to hold together in one Church people who engage with God in different ways, and come from distinct spiritual traditions.

In other Christian denominations there might be greater uniformity and a particular way of doing things in church that has become '*the* way' of doing things. However, as discussed in Chapter 1, Anglican churches have certain central teachings in common, but diversity in the style of worship is to be expected and embraced. Differences in worship style are particularly evident in the Church of England, but the same occurs in Anglican Churches all around the world.

I remember being slightly shocked when an American priest doused me with holy water before we processed in to take a Sunday service. And my more 'Reformed' church origins were again exposed in another Episcopalian 'Mass', where my friend 'Father Phil' – a real mountain of a man – had to resort to turning my body to face the right direction at particular moments in the service. Hilariously for the congregation, he found that pushing his Goliath-like hands down on my shoulders was the most effective way to get me to genuflect (that is, kneel) at the appropriate moments during the 'Mass'.

Sadly, the differences in worship style and spirituality are not always viewed positively. I can think of several countries in South America where heated discussions on 'Anglican identity' have threatened to drive a wedge between parishes, dioceses and even Provinces. This unfortunate 'us' and 'them' scenario can occur anywhere, with issues around human sexuality sometimes reinforcing difference and divisions.

Ultimately, whether it's in the American Midwest, the rural English village, the Caribbean sands or the snowy Canadian mountains, the person who compares St Chad's and St Mary's and asks 'Who's got it *right*?' has got it wrong, because they're simply asking the wrong question. A more traditional 'bells and smells' approach at St Saviour's is in terms of Anglican tradition just as valid as the approach taken by St Peter's where there are no such trimmings. Revd Kev's 30-minute biblical exposition has a very different feel from Revd Ted's five-minute homily, but both priests are sincere and take as a given that Scripture carries divine authority and is to be heard, digested and reflected on by God's people.

Father Bob leads from the front with his back to the congregation, but it's not because he's so rude and stressed out that he can't bear to look at the people sitting in the pews. Bob has his back to the congregation because like a contemporary Moses figure he is leading God's people forward on their journey towards the promised land of holiness and encounter with the living Christ. He is referred to as 'Father' because the more Catholic tradition refers to the bishop and priest as 'Father in God' out of deference, and in order to underline his pastoral – almost paternal – presence and responsibility towards the congregation.

The issues raised in relation to our fictional but true-to-life churches are to do with church tradition, sometimes known – in ponderous and politically incorrect language – as 'churchmanship'. Today, 500 years after the Reformation, the coexistence of parish churches from different ends of the Catholic–Reformed spectrum is the outworking of the inclusive and conciliatory

Anglican ethos. Globally, there is a Catholic wing to Anglicanism just as there is a more Reformed wing. The former is often referred to as 'high' church whereas the latter is dubbed 'low' church. If someone asks 'How high up the candle are you?' it's not that they're on hallucinatory drugs – or even that they suspect *you* are. Rather, they're asking you a question about church tradition and where you sit on the Catholic–Reformed scale.

It is a fact that for roughly ten centuries British Christianity was largely Roman Catholic, and it is therefore not surprising that in spite of the Reformation the Church of England – and indeed the Anglican Communion – is both shaped by and has retained elements of Catholicism. In Roman Catholic countries in South America it is not unusual for Catholics to enter Anglican churches believing the priest to be a 'padre' leading a Roman Catholic Mass. Some Anglicans, of course, would welcome the identification and, ever since the 'Oxford Movement' (see Chapter 7), sectors of Anglicanism have sought to recover and revive the historic connection between Canterbury and Rome.[6]

In Chapter 1 we saw how 'word' and 'sacrament' are absolutely central to Anglican identity. While theologians from both ends of the spectrum stress the importance of 'word' and 'sacrament', more Reformed Anglicans might gravitate towards the 'word', whereas more Catholic Anglicans might tend towards 'sacrament'. The two ends of the Catholic–Reformed spectrum might be illustrated as in Table 1.

Table 1	
Word	*Sacrament*
Reformed (evangelical)	Catholic
Low church	High church

6 There is even a group known as the Anglican–Roman Catholic International Commission (ARCIC), which for 50 years has worked to bring Anglicans and Roman Catholics into closer fellowship. For further information, see: http://www.anglicancommunion.org/relationships/ecumenical-dialogues/roman-catholic/arcic.aspx.

Returning to our fictional but true-to-life churches, the fact that St Chad's have a Bible-based message every Sunday but 'do Communion' just once a month may suggest a strong leaning towards 'word', with just a nod towards 'sacrament'. On the other hand, St Mary's 'celebrate Mass' several times a week so there is plenty of 'sacrament', but the priest's two-minute 'thought for the day' soundbite suggests a weak presence of 'word'. However, both churches – in their different ways – would consider they were being faithful to Anglican practice and heritage. St Chad's gravitates to the 'word' and Reformed (evangelical) end of the spectrum and can be described as 'low church', and St Mary's sits at the 'sacrament' and Catholic end and might be described as 'high church'.

These are caricatures but they give a clue as to how a particular church can inhabit the Catholic sacramental end of the scale or the Reformed and biblical end. Though churches might sit at opposite ends of the Catholic–Reformed spectrum, there are sometimes emphases in common. For instance, since the 1950s and 1960s, in the UK the so-called 'charismatic movement' has usually been associated with the evangelical wing of the Church. Nevertheless, in the USA and some South American countries an openness to experiencing the Holy Spirit and actively pursuing and exercising spiritual gifts – particularly prophecy and speaking in tongues – is not uncommon in Anglican Catholic circles.[7] Thus, the spectrum of church tradition might be modified as in Table 2.

Table 2	
Word	Sacrament
Reformed (evangelical)	Catholic
Low church	High church
Charismatic	Charismatic

---

7 In the Church of England, the annual 'On Fire' conference similarly combines charismatic and Catholic approaches to spirituality, cf. https://www. onfiremission.org.

The same is true, but in reverse, when it comes to a 'contemplative' spirituality. Thus, in the Church of England it is not unusual to find evangelical churches incorporating contemplative styles of worship and prayer – for example, tapping into the rich vein of Celtic spirituality – when such approaches originate in, and are characteristic of, certain religious orders and a more Catholic approach. It is often the case that the evangelical churches that accommodate more contemplative spirituality – for example, Taizé services, *lectio divina* – are also those with charismatic tendencies.

Returning once more to our fictional parishes, we read earlier that St Martin's 'won't have a woman vicar' whereas Revd Sheila down at St Matthew's is well loved by her congregation. Several Anglican Provinces, covering regions such as the USA, Mexico, Japan, Uganda, North and South India, Australia, and latterly the Church of England, admit women to the three orders of ordained ministry (deacon, priest, bishop). On the other hand, there are Provinces in the Anglican Communion – for example, the Southern Cone in South America – where women are not eligible to be ordained either as priest or bishop. Make-believe St Martin's that won't have a woman priest could either be a low church conservative evangelical parish, or equally it could be a high church Anglo-Catholic parish, as illustrated in Table 3.

Table 3	
Word	*Sacrament*
Reformed (evangelical)	Catholic
Low church	High church
Conservative	Anglo-Catholic

If St Martin's were a low church of conservative evangelical persuasion, then the reasons for not having a woman priest would be connected to an interpretation of the Bible that holds to a strict view of 'male headship'. This position is commonly called 'complementarianism' as those who hold it argue that men and women have different but complementary roles in church leadership. While such churches might welcome women leaders and allow them to become deacons, they believe that the biblical teaching and precedent requires exclusively male presbyters (elders) or priests – at least as the 'vicar' or 'priest in charge' of the parish.

On the other hand, if St Martin's were a high-church, traditional Anglo-Catholic parish, then the reasons for insisting on exclusively male priests would be as much to do with maintaining the tradition of the Church and its apostolicity as about following a biblical precedent. They would urge that Jesus' 12 apostles were male, and throughout its history the clergy have been male and that this is a tradition that must be respected and upheld.

In the main, both conservative evangelicals and Anglo-Catholics also hold traditional views on marriage and sexuality. Thus, some conservative evangelicals and some Anglo-Catholics – who are miles apart in terms of their spirituality – stand together within the conservative global Anglican movement known as GAFCON.[8]

Just down the road from St Martin's is St Matthew's, where Revd Sheila is much loved by her parishioners. Again, we would need to know more about St Matthew's in order to work out where it sits on the Catholic–Reformed spectrum. Clearly, since the congregation have embraced a woman priest, St Matthew's is not a conservative evangelical parish, nor is it likely to be traditional Anglo-Catholic. It could, however, be a *charismatic* church of some description, or again, it might be what is known in the UK as an 'open' evangelical church. The 'open' evangelical tradition welcomes women to all three orders of ordained ministry. It claims to be biblically rooted and seeks to make sense of Scripture in dialogue with culture and contemporary issues. On issues such as homosexuality, for example, 'open evangelicals' are committed

---

8 GAFCON stands for 'Global Anglican Future Conference' as the movement was born out of a conference held in Jerusalem in 2008 (cf. https://www.gafcon.org).

to conversations with 'progressives' and 'conservatives'. Some will be reasonably 'open' to the possibility of bringing radical change to current ecclesiastical practices; others will be more cautious and less 'open' – a tension that shows how misleading these labels can become.[9]

On the other hand, St Matthew's could equally be a 'liberal Catholic church' – in other words, a church that has a strongly sacramental and liturgical orientation, but that maintains an open, progressive approach to questions about women in ministry and sexuality. In contrast to the conservative evangelical alignment with the GAFCON movement, liberal Catholics often identify with the 'Affirming Catholicism' movement, and with pro-gay initiatives such as 'Inclusive Church' and the 'LGBTI Anglican Coalition'.[10] As in the other Anglican traditions, while it is rightly categorized in Table 4 under 'Sacrament', Scripture is nevertheless a key element of liberal Catholic theology and spirituality, where there is a concern to bring it into conversation with the contemporary world. Thus, as well as an emphasis on personal holiness, a key strength is the application of a biblical perspective to issues in social justice. Thus, in the case of the liberal Catholic tradition, the Catholic–Reformed spectrum would be modified as in Table 4.

Table 4	
Word	Sacrament
Reformed (evangelical)	Catholic
Low church	High church
Open Evangelical	Liberal Catholic

---

9 For a fascinating discussion of the different strands of Anglican evangelicalism, see Graham Kings, 'Canal, River and Rapids: Contemporary Evangelicalism in the Church of England', *Anvil*, 20.3, 2003, pp. 167–84, available at: https://www.fulcrum-anglican.org.uk/articles/canal-river-and-rapids-contemporary-evangelicalism-in-the-church-of-england.

10 See further, for 'Affirming Catholicism': http://www.affirmingcatholicism.org.uk; for 'Inclusive Church': https://inclusive-church.org; and for 'LGBTI Anglican Coalition': http://www.lgbtianglican.org.uk.

On the whole, Anglican churches seldom lend themselves to these simple black and white caricatures. This is especially true in the Church of England, where we even have a label for the churches that don't fit neatly into any other category – namely, 'middle of the road'! Other than giving a sense that the worship is probably on the traditional side, 'middle of the road' could mean virtually anything. This shows that the clear-cut categorization set out in Tables 1–4 functions for illustrative purposes, but shouldn't be pressed too far. In Anglicanism, 'word' and 'sacrament' are meant to be held together, not apart, so on the ground we should expect to find a good deal of convergence and overlap between traditions.

On my travels I have found evangelical Anglican churches that stress the authority of Scripture (often called a 'high view of Scripture'), but maintain an equally 'high view of the sacraments' and follow a pattern of Sunday and midweek Eucharistic services. But I have encountered Anglo-Catholic churches and priests who have an extremely 'high view of Scripture' also and are strongly biblical. When I was on the clergy team of a Brazilian cathedral we tried to combine a strong Bible focus with a vibrant sacramental approach within a charismatic and contemplative worship style.

The question of church traditions and Anglican spirituality does come with a health warning, though. There can be a danger of *tribalism* when discussing church traditions. All too often labels such as 'evangelical' and 'liberal' can be verbal hand grenades tossed in to conversation to wound and pigeonhole people we disagree with. An 'us' versus 'them' mentality sadly darkens discussions around Anglican identity and fuels an unhealthy obsession that treats one particular tradition as if it were the only *true* expression of Anglicanism.

Things become especially confusing on the international stage as particular terms mean different things to different people depending on their context. For example, 'evangelical' means one thing in England but quite another in the USA, and something else again in South America. Even the word 'Anglican' has become politically loaded in the USA where the Anglican Church in North America (ACNA) has emerged in opposition to, and distinction from, The Episcopal Church (TEC) over the issue of homosexuality and the Church.

Nevertheless, we're unlikely to shake off labels such as 'liberal', 'evangelical', 'Catholic' and 'charismatic', and they do have a limited usefulness for getting a broad handle on the different strands of church tradition that are woven together in the world-wide Anglican Church.

So, why does the parish down the road do things so differently?

This chapter has explored the topic of Anglican church traditions, sometimes referred to in non-PC language as 'churchmanship'. We have seen how, since the Reformation, the Church of England has self-identified as the Church of and for the people, seeking to be inclusive of different perspectives and approaches to worship. Similarly, in Anglican Churches throughout the world various ways of worship coexist, and though they may look and feel very different to one another each tradition has its place and its unique contribution.

Questions for individual or group reflection

1 Reflect on your own experience of Anglican churches. How would you describe the 'tradition' of the church you currently attend?
2 In what sense has the history of the Church of England set the coordinates for a diverse spectrum of 'churchmanship' in global Anglicanism?
3 What does the way in which a particular church worships tell you about their approach to spirituality?

4 Are there any elements that a church must have if it is to be *authentically* Anglican? If so, what are they?
5 If you are able, why not visit a different Anglican church that has a tradition that is different from your own? What do you most value about the way the other church worships God, and what (if anything) do you find difficult or odd?

3

What's the point of liturgy?

From my schooldays I recall a discussion with a friend from the Brethren Church who was adamant that our Anglican liturgy comprises the very kind of 'vain repetition' that Jesus had warned against in the Sermon on the Mount.[1] I wasn't sure how to respond to that slightly troubling contention back then, but now I would point out that the emphasis of the Greek words falls on the vanity or *emptiness* of the *many* words rather than on 'repetition' per se. The contrast drawn by Jesus in Matthew 6.6–7 is actually between the empty gabbling of idol worshippers and the purposeful prayer of those who know God as Father.

'Purposeful prayer' is quite a good way of answering the question about the point of liturgy. While the etymology of the term has to do with the *work* carried out in togetherness by the community, 'liturgy' has come to be defined more narrowly as the pattern of worship and prayer that orders a church service. In this sense, every church uses liturgy in its public acts of worship. Even the most informal expressions of Christian worship follow some kind of order, albeit a loose one, perhaps including a time of sung worship, a Bible reading and a short talk.

When Moses approached God in his awesome holiness he was instructed to remove his sandals on entering holy ground (Exodus 3.5). As we come before our God who is the definition of holiness, pure love and all that is thoroughly good, our liturgy helps focus our hearts and our worship. We might arrive at a service joyfully pumped up with a thousand thanks to give to God.

---

[1] Occasionally this kind of accusation is still levelled at Anglicans, particularly in predominantly Roman Catholic countries where Pentecostal churches are suspicious of anything that resembles Catholic ritual.

Equally, though, in the grip of loss, disappointment or depression, we might struggle even to make it to and through the church door. Either way, the liturgy signposts us to God, orders our thoughts and helps situate the events and emotions of our lives in the context of divine care.

If we track back to the apostle Paul's instructions in 1 Corinthians 14, we find a connection between liturgy, orderly worship and the proper exercising of spiritual gifts. The church in Corinth was about as dysfunctional as any church could be, so arguably it needed a good dose of 'order and decency' (cf. 1 Corinthians 14.40), and a real shake-up. But since every congregation consists of normal people who get things wrong as well as right, in all cases a structured approach to worship helps restore the spiritual balance. Just as God brings order to our chaotic world, the service of worship is very often the place where his Spirit orders and reorders our lives through and in Christ. The opportunities for stillness and silent reflection that our Anglican liturgies afford can be an important part of this reordering encounter with God. Others will find that sung worship ignites their souls and allows them to reconnect with the Lord. Many become aware that Holy Communion allows for a spiritual 're-set' as Jesus becomes present to them in that special moment.

On a practical level the liturgy is there to facilitate worship, to help us offer and (re)commit our lives to God in prayer and praise. The person leading the worship brings the congregation before God in togetherness and has a special responsibility, captured nicely in Izaak Walton's seventeenth-century verse:

> He that unto others leads the way
> In public prayer,
> Should do it so,
> As all, that hear, may know
> They need not fear
> To tune their hearts unto his tongue, and say
> Amen.[2]

---

2 Izaak Walton, *The Compleat Angler*, New York: Modern Library, 1939 (1653), p. 136.

As the congregation 'tune their hearts' to the words of the service, the liturgy moves through phases and is deliberately structured to draw us in to contemplate the deep mysteries of divine grace. In this sense our liturgies provide a ready-made framework for worship, but also help form the very substance of that act of praise and thanksgiving to God. The set words and prayers aid the verbalization of what is on our hearts and minds. The Scripture readings are a source of spiritual encouragement and affirmation, of comfort or of challenge.

While my friends from a Free Church background may suspect that the Anglican liturgy is over-formulaic and too prosaic, restricting freedom in worship and curbing genuine reflection, nothing could be further from the truth. (The term 'Free Church' refers to Churches separate from the 'established' Church; Free Churches have no ties to the government of the nation.) Our Anglican liturgy builds in space for quiet personal reflection and can employ a variety of prayers and service forms, not to mention Eucharistic prayers. Times of intercession allow us to bring particular concerns freely before God. Even set pieces such as 'The Peace' in the service of Holy Communion can be slotted in at different points and the shape of a service is not rigidly fixed.

It's true that set prayers offer familiarity, which Anglicans appreciate as they point to their core identity in Christ as well as to the basic principles of faith. Indeed, the liturgy takes us back to the familiar and basic building blocks of our Christian faith – such as the Lord's Prayer – and this enables us to refocus on God's priorities for us and for the world. Nevertheless, services of Anglican worship should not become stale because familiarity is counterbalanced by variety in the form of seasonal prefaces, collects and prayers. Our Anglican liturgies are fairly comprehensive and, when used well, provide a healthy, creative mix of familiarity and variety in worship. Clergy, and those involved in preparing and delivering services, have a large degree of freedom to craft worship in different ways. I believe it was Bishop Hippolytus in the early period of Christianity who stressed that the liturgy is a valuable tool to be used creatively in the hand of God's people and ministers – it is our servant rather than our master.

In the words of the old hymn, our Eucharistic liturgies 'tell the wondrous story of the Christ who died for me'. More generally, Anglican liturgy revisits the great truths of the Christian faith as communicated to us in Scripture. In this way it reminds us of the great biblical story of the people of God, highlighting key themes such as liberation, wilderness wanderings, forgiveness, salvation, restoration, covenant and the firm hope of a bright future with God. The re-telling of the Christian story situates us as God's people within his plans and purposes and within salvation history. It reminds us of the wider narrative of salvation in which we have our place and our part to play today. The following prayer of thanksgiving from the Church of England's Common Worship series illustrates these characteristics in a memorable way:

> Blessed are you, Sovereign Lord, the God and Father of our Lord Jesus Christ, to you be glory and praise for ever. From the deep waters of death you brought your people to new birth by raising your Son to life in triumph. Through him dark death has been destroyed and radiant life is everywhere restored. As you call us out of darkness into his marvellous light may our lives reflect his glory and our lips repeat the endless song. Blessed be God, Father, Son and Holy Spirit. Blessed be God for ever.[3]

As the reference to Jesus being raised to life suggests, seasonally this prayer belongs to the Easter season. Notice how the prayer hints at the Exodus theme of passing through the Red Sea but links this to our own new birth, effected by Jesus' resurrection: 'From the deep waters of death you brought your people to new birth by raising your Son to life in triumph.' Different strands of the overarching biblical story are skilfully woven together – liberation, new birth in Christ (with baptism in mind), and resurrection victory.

---

3 *Common Worship: Daily Prayer*, London: Church House Publishing, 2005, p. 269.

The next lines poetically allude to the destruction of 'dark death' and the restoration of 'radiant life'. First and foremost, following on from the reference to Jesus' resurrection, this reminds us of the empty tomb and the apostle Paul's triumphant cry 'Death has lost its sting!' The Easter events are the story of salvation embedded within the broader salvation story of God bringing light and life to humanity amid the darkness and death. We might find echoes here of God as creator who brings light and life. Perhaps we call to mind Isaiah's prophecies concerning the Servant of the Lord who is a 'light to the Gentiles' but, above all, we are powerfully reminded of the beginning of John's Gospel, not least the state-ment: '... in him [Jesus] was life, and the life was the light of all people. The light shines in the darkness, and the darkness has not overcome it' (John 1.4–5).

As explained above, our liturgies are especially helpful in placing *our lives* within God's unfolding plan for humanity. Objective statements about Jesus' saving work and power now take on a subjective application: 'As you call *us* out of darkness into his marvellous light, may *our* lives reflect his glory and *our* lips repeat the endless song' (emphasis mine). Our Anglican liturgies are far from abstract or detached academic pronouncements: rather, there is a very practical 'DIY' dimension to them.

Thus, in a short opening prayer, our thoughts have been directed to God's saving acts described in the Old Testament and to the ultimate saving act of God – namely, the death and resurrection of Jesus Christ. After stating the biblical truth that Jesus has destroyed 'dark death' the prayer then confronts us with the out-working and meaning of this for our own lives today. The note of praise and thanksgiving that is sounded at the start of the prayer returns at its close. In this way, the entire storytelling is framed by explicit acknowledgement of the blessedness of God the Father, Son and Holy Spirit.

By telling and re-telling the salvation story and by underlining our place in God's plans, our Anglican liturgies affirm our Christian identity. In church, our collective responses and prayers help us *talk the talk* but the liturgy also challenges us to *walk the walk* – that is, to live each day for Jesus. The *common* prayers and service orders that were written from the time of the Reformation have universal appeal and are of relevance for all Anglicans. Our 'collects' gather us together as one people in an attitude of worship, and the 'dismissal' sends us out into the world as one people united in Christ, voicing a shared intention to live for God. Our confessional liturgies recognize the common thread of human fallenness just as our prayers of absolution (the declaration of forgiveness of sins, made by a priest in God's name) recognize the forgiveness of sins freely offered to all those who are open to God with penitent hearts. Our Eucharistic prayers include congregational responses that further point to our group identity as the gathered people of God.

It emerges from this that the collective, community aspect of Anglican liturgy is a defining characteristic. Wherever possible, Anglican clergy are encouraged to pray the Daily Offices – that is, the set daily prayers for Morning Prayer and Evening Prayer – in acts of public worship. Practically, unless one is based in a cathedral or a religious community such as a monastery where services are held throughout the day, the Daily Offices are often said in private at home. Even then, though, it is inspiring and comforting to know that Anglican brothers and sisters around the world are also praying and worshipping in this way, and the daily intercessions are an invitation to consider the wider Christian community and world, committing these to God's care. Of course, you needn't be ordained to pray through the Daily Office each day. The Church of England's Daily Prayer App is a fantastic tool that allows people to take 10–15 minutes wherever they are just to stop what they are doing and offer prayer and praise.

Though many Provinces in the Anglican Communion have translated versions of the English liturgy, they are also free to commission and produce their own liturgies.[4] In this way, Angli-

4 Since the nineteenth century, though, overseas Churches have been asked to carefully consider what effect any 'revisions' to the Prayer Book might have

can worship is grounded in tradition, but also contextualized in a way that particular cultures can comprehend. In the north-east of Brazil, for instance, a seasonal Anglican prayer form adopts the distinctive speech rhythms of a type of rural folk music known as 'cordel'. The content of the liturgy focuses on thanksgiving for God's creation as it is used in the season of the corn harvest. The resulting liturgy appeals to the people in so far as its rhythms are identifiable and culturally determined while the substance of the prayers tallies with the time of year.

So far, we have seen that the point of liturgy as 'purposeful prayer' is to order and facilitate our public and private worship of God. It provides the framework for worship, but as the verbalization in prayer of our feelings, thoughts, concerns and longings it also shapes and articulates the substance of our worship. The familiarity of set phrases and prayers reminds us of our core Christian identity. Variety in symbol, song and statement, especially in terms of the cyclical seasons of the Christian calendar, helps us look at aspects of our faith with fresh eyes and hear eternal truths with eager ears. In so far as our liturgy recaps and restates the Christian story, it enables us to refocus on our identity in Christ and encourages us to play our part as messengers and servants of God in the overarching salvation story. While some find solace and joy in praying ancient prayers in their original Book of Common Prayer form, contemporary liturgies such as the Church of England's Common Worship series preserve the essence of the traditional prayers while providing more accessible and modern language. Anglican Churches overseas compose their own liturgies in a way that honours the central truths of our faith, while also capturing prayer and praise in culturally relevant forms.

---

on other Churches in the Anglican Communion – see, for example, Resolution 10 of the Lambeth Conference of 1888: http://www.anglicancommunion.org/resources/document-library/lambeth-conference/1888/resolution-10.aspx.

Liturgy and theology

One of the classically Anglican emphases to do with liturgy is the principle enshrined in the Latin phrase *lex orandi, lex credendi* – roughly translated, *the stuff we pray is the stuff we believe*. Once more, the claim sometimes made that the Anglican Church has 'no doctrine' overlooks the fact that our liturgy is the living expression of our core beliefs. Saturated in Scripture, Anglican liturgy makes definitive statements about the character of God. 'Merciful Father', 'Gracious Lord', 'Almighty God' and 'Holy Lord' are a small smattering of summary statements that encapsulate and flag up larger doctrinal considerations based on the character of God as revealed in the Bible.

Starting with the Book of Common Prayer, masterminded by Archbishop Cranmer and revised in 1662, our liturgy underlines Anglicanism's commitment to a Trinitarian understanding of God. Traditionally, Anglican services of worship begin with explicit reference to the triune God; thus, the priest may introduce a service by saying: 'In the name of the Father, and of the Son and of the Holy Spirit'. Therefore, the invocation of God the Holy Trinity sets the tone for acts of worship. Prayers are directed to God the Father in the name of God the Son and in the power of God the Holy Spirit. Just before the people of God are sent out into the world to live for the glory of God, the priest prays a blessing over them, a blessing that is explicitly Trinitarian – for example, 'The blessing of God the Father, God the Son and God the Holy Spirit be upon you and remain with you always'.

Anglican liturgy, then, focuses our minds and hearts on the God whom we profess and serve. It makes important statements about who we believe God to be, and these are informed by our understanding of God as revealed in Scripture and human history. The Eucharistic liturgies in particular celebrate the character of God with adjectives such as 'gracious', 'merciful' and 'loving' in the light of our understanding of Jesus' death and resurrection as the supreme saving act of God.

The theology of atonement – that is, the Christian understanding and interpretation of the sacrificial death of Jesus – is multi-layered and speaks to us in many ways. Different parts of our Eucharistic prayers focus on different aspects of the cross. It is usually the case that the liturgy will allude to the 'once for all' sacrifice made by Jesus for us. Similarly, mention is normally made of Jesus' death having the effect of purifying and cleansing us from sin. Some prayers speak of Jesus 'rescuing us from sin and death', others use technical-sounding words such as 'redemption', 'justification' and 'propitiation'.[5] Eucharistic prayers tend also to speak of the resurrection, explaining that Jesus' rising from the dead to new life ensures that we also have new life, being 'dead to sin' and 'alive in Christ'.

As explained above, in telling and re-telling the Christian story, Anglican liturgies highlight our identity as the people of God. Within this, just as statements are made about the character and nature of God, there are reflections on humanity and what it means to be human. Our confessional prayers, for instance, recognize the universal tendency to make a mess of relationships and to turn away from God. On the other hand, there are also statements about the healing of relationships and humanity realizing its creative potential in Christ. Again, the priestly administering of a prayer of absolution can be a very powerful restorative moment for a person who is deeply convicted of the grievousness of a particular attitude or act of wrongdoing.

---

5 'Redemption' is a term that derives from the slave markets in New Testament times and means that by dying on the cross Jesus paid the price in order to free us from 'slavery to sin'. 'Justification' is a term with a legal background; it means that by taking upon himself our wrongdoing and thinking, Jesus frees us of any punishment that the divine judge might otherwise level against us. 'Propitiation' is to do with retribution – where an offended party exacts punishment on an individual – and it means that at the cross the righteous anger of God against evil focuses on Jesus (rather than humankind) as he bears the sin of humanity.

Spreading the net wider, our prayers of intercession and Anglican litanies – that is, a series of prayers – indicate that we long to see the coming of God's kingdom on earth and the flourishing of the common good. Every sphere of earthly life is offered over to God in prayer, from rulers and governors of nations to local authorities, communities and the needs of particular individuals known to us personally. The Church worldwide is upheld in prayer, as are its leaders and members. I think of the structure of intercessory prayers in concentric circles: the outer circle represents prayer for the wider world, for world leaders and for peace and harmony throughout the globe. As we move inwards, the focus becomes the land in which we live, the governors of our nation and for the Church in our country. Again, the next circle homes in on our local congregation and community and, finally, in the centre we pray for ourselves, our families and friends and those people who lead and guide us in our faith in the regional and local church.

The English Reformers were well aware that the liturgy has a didactic dimension. In other words, liturgy can become a powerful teaching tool for instructing people in the core beliefs of the faith. As in some Anglican Churches in Africa and South America today, during the Reformation many people were illiterate or had very limited literacy skills. The repetition of set prayers and statements of liturgical worship imprints on the heart and mind the central truths of Christianity. Today, some prayers and Eucharistic liturgies have a very practical feel to them. One Eucharistic prayer from Kenya has been used in several countries – I have come across it in both Portuguese and Spanish translation – and I think it gives us a sense of the liturgy as a teaching tool. The opening part of the prayer is as follows:

Celebrant: Is the Father with us?
People: **He is.**
Celebrant: Is Christ among us?
People: **He is.**
Celebrant: Is the Spirit here?
People: **He is.**

Celebrant: This is our God:
People: **Father, Son and Holy Spirit.**
Celebrant: We are his people:
People: **We are redeemed.**
Celebrant: Lift up your hearts:
People: **We lift them to the Lord.**
Celebrant: Let us give thanks to the Lord our God:
People: **It is right to give him thanks and praise.**[6]

This question and answer form is reminiscent of catechesis, the ancient practice of learning the basics of Christianity by way of a series of questions and short responses, still used in Roman Catholicism today and recently revived by the Church of England in its publication *The Pilgrim Way*.[7] The Kenyan prayer is highly memorable and a very effective way of conveying and absorbing the central truths of Christian belief. In terms of its content, in pithy, concise language Anglican identity is rooted in the context of a relationship with God the Father through Christ the Son. Later in the prayer, after the priest has spoken the words of institution – that is, the part that repeats Jesus' words about the bread representing his body and the wine his blood – the people again respond with a statement that anchors and celebrates their shared identity in Christ: 'Amen, We are brothers and sisters through his blood. We have died together. We will rise together. We will live together.' Simple, yes, but beautifully simple and simply beautiful.

Liturgy, season and symbol

For Anglicans, because the liturgy accompanies the changing seasons, it forms part of the rhythm and fabric of life. For northern hemisphere Anglicans, the quadrants of the 'liturgical year' are intimately linked to the cycles of nature: Easter goes hand in hand with spring, whereas Advent and Christmas call to mind

---

6 This and the next citations are from Global Anglican Theological Institute: http//globalanglican.wordpress.com/a-kenyan-liturgy, accessed 5 May 2017.

7 Information on *The Pilgrim Way* can be found at www.churchofengland.org.

scenes of winter. As mentioned above, within what is known as the 'liturgical calendar', collects and prayers are worded in ways that invite reflection on themes linked to the season.[8]

Reflections on Scripture in the form of 'scriptural sentences' – that is, short quotations from the Bible – are also appropriate to the liturgical calendar. Meaningful theological words feature in the set prayers for particular seasons – for example, 'Alleluia' (defined as 'praise the Lord') in the Easter season to celebrate the resurrection, 'Maranatha', an Aramaic word meaning 'come, Lord Jesus', in Advent, anticipating the coming of Jesus. The lectionary – that is, the Anglican cycle of set Bible readings – should also bear some relation to the liturgical calendar, though the connections are sometimes subtle.

Here is an example of a seasonal prayer and a couple of scriptural sentences from the Church of England's Common Worship liturgy used in Morning Prayer in the weeks after Easter and before Pentecost:

Blessed are you, Lord God of our salvation, to you be praise and glory for ever. As once you ransomed your people from Egypt and led them to freedom in the promised land, so now you have delivered us from the dominion of darkness and brought us into the kingdom of your risen Son. May we, the first fruits of your new creation, rejoice in this new day you have made, and praise you for your mighty acts. Blessed be God, Father, Son and Holy Spirit.

Christ has been raised from the dead: the first fruits of those who sleep. For as by man came death; by man has come also the resurrection of the dead; for as in Adam all die: even so in Christ shall all be made alive (Romans 6.9–11).[9]

---

8 For a concise and accessible treatment of this, see David Kennedy, *Using Common Worship: Times and Seasons*, London: Church House Publishing, 2006.

9 *Common Worship: Daily Prayer*, London: Church House Publishing, 2005, p. 263.

By drawing on and revisiting prayers that follow the themes linked to a particular festival or season, Anglicans are able to reflect on biblical and spiritual truths over a period of time. In other Churches important dates like Christmas or Easter might be celebrated just before the big day, and then on the big day itself. These big occasions tend to be hyper-busy both at home and church. The advantage of the Anglican approach is that prayerful reflection about the meaning of the season both precedes and follows the big day. When it is used intentionally and consistently, the liturgy, then, gives Anglicans the chance to get to grips with the foundational moments of Christianity as expressed in the liturgical year.

While the words of our Anglican prayer books form the mainstay of our liturgies, liturgy also involves symbols, colours and gestures. Just as the words used in worship are tailored to the season, so the colour scheme follows the liturgical calendar. For example, white is used at Christmas and Easter, and on special or holy days, and it represents the purity and holiness of God. Green is used during 'ordinary time' – that is, the periods of the year that fall between the festival times. It is often thought to point to creation and the goodness of our Creator God. The colour red appears on priestly vestments and on the Lord's Table at Pentecost. The vivid vibrancy of bright red represents both the life-giving richness of the Holy Spirit and the tongues of fire that rested on Jesus' followers on the Day of Pentecost (cf. Acts 2). On special days when the lives of Christian martyrs are commemorated red is also used, but in this case it represents the blood of the martyrs spilt for the cause of the gospel. Other liturgical colours include purple, which in the ancient world symbolized royalty, majesty and authority. It is apt that purple is used in Advent since during this time we celebrate Jesus' coming into the world as the royal Messiah and King of kings. Purple, though, has another connotation at a different time in the liturgical year. During Lent, the 40-day period preceding Easter, purple again symbolizes a time of waiting and expectation, but in this case it is linked to an attitude of repentance and turning away from sin; dark blue may also be used and carries the same meaning.

There is a similar liturgical richness around the furniture and fittings of the church building. For instance, in many churches the font for baptism is located near to the entrance. This is deliberate and signifies the *entrance* of the newly baptized person into the family of faith. Stained-glass windows tell stories about the faithfulness of God through the ages and hold up examples of faithful Christian people. Banners that adorn pillars and walls are very often loaded with Christian symbols, some of which might also appear on priestly vestments, such as a Greek Alpha and Omega, reminding us of the words in Revelation and the amazing reality that Jesus is 'the First and the Last' or 'the beginning and the end' – the centre of all life.

While different church traditions draw to varying extents on liturgical symbolism, some features are very common throughout the Anglican Communion and appear in most churches. An obvious place to start would be the Lord's Table set for Holy Communion where a collection of vessels and cloths are set out on and around the elements of bread and wine. In the Anglo-Catholic tradition each cloth and vessel has a special meaning pertaining to aspects of Jesus' sacrifice – for example, the corporal is a square white linen cloth that recalls the sheet in which Jesus' body lay. Another very common item are candles. Cathedrals often reserve a space where people can light a candle and say a prayer. Candles symbolize God's light and recall John 1.5: 'The light shines in the darkness, and the darkness has not overcome it.' In many Anglican churches there is a large paschal candle which is lit for services of Holy Baptism. The priest will light a smaller candle from the large candle and give it to the newly baptized person or to their family. The smaller candle is then carried out of the sanctuary and the story-told-by-symbol is complete: Jesus is the light of the world, his light kindles our hearts that we may shine, and this involves going out and taking his light into the world.

In addition to symbols, Anglican liturgy is also characterized by gestures. Typically, these are visible actions that indicate reverence towards God. Thus, in some church traditions within Anglicanism it is the norm to make the sign of the cross – for instance, before receiving Holy Communion. Again, when consecrating the bread and wine during the Eucharist, the priest may sign the cross over them and, when giving his or her priestly blessing at the end of a service, may make the sign of the cross. Genuflection (bowing the knee in reverence) is another common gesture in some Anglican traditions, and Anglo-Catholic priests will tend to do this at particular moments during the Eucharistic prayer.

Sometimes the meaning of a gesture is fairly self-explanatory – for example, when an offertory plate is raised up after the collection it is clear that the gifts of money are being offered to God above. Again, laying hands on people in prayer is a gesture that requires little explanation, provided people know the biblical background to this – that is, the Holy Spirit is invited to fill someone with a view to carrying out a particular role or task or sometimes to heal them. For the benefit of newcomers or visitors, though, when the laying on of hands is done as a special commissioning by a bishop in a service of confirmation or ordination the words of the liturgy help unpack the underlying significance of that laying on of hands.

On the other hand, the meaning behind some gestures or actions may not be immediately apparent to the congregation. Thus, some church traditions maintain the tradition of having the Gospel reading in the chancel. This is to show that the gospel, and by extension Christ himself, becomes present and *dwells* in the midst of the people. Again, newcomers to more traditional Anglican churches find that when saying the Creed people seem to turn their bodies at an angle. The reason for doing this might not be obvious, but there is a point to it – namely, to face eastwards in respectful recognition that it was in the East where these events came to pass and where these truths were revealed.

So, what's the point of liturgy, again?

This chapter has discussed the Anglican liturgy and has offered a working definition of 'liturgy' as 'purposeful prayer'. The point of liturgy, as we have seen, is to order and organize our worship of the God who brings order to chaos. Our liturgies provide a framework for worship but they also bring substance, colour, life and direction to our prayers and services. In telling and re-telling the story of the people of God our liturgies help root our personal and collective stories within his salvation story.

By reminding us of the basics of the Christian faith, the liturgy also has a didactic function, etching God's word into our hearts and minds. Again, in so far as it communicates God's truth through symbolism, our Anglican liturgy helps us appreciate more who God is and who we are in Christ.

Questions for individual or group reflection

1 Is it true to say that *all* Christian Churches, Anglican or otherwise, use some form of liturgy?
2 What would be your response to the person who is suspicious that Anglican liturgy falls into the category of 'vain repetition'?
3 Reflect on the cyclical nature of Anglican liturgy. Are there particular seasons in which you notice liturgical symbols and traditions? What are these and what is so special about them?
4 How does your personal faith story fit into the overall story of God's faithfulness through history?
5 What have you learnt about Anglican symbolism in this chapter, and is this something you might want to find out more about by chatting to a member of the clergy?

4

What are the essentials of Anglican theology?

Contrary to popular belief, the Anglican Church was not founded by Henry VIII. Rather, as part of the one catholic (that is, universal) and apostolic Church, Jesus himself is both the founder and the foundation of the Anglican Church. Together with Christians all over the world from all kinds of church backgrounds, Anglicans are part of 'the Church' that traces its origins to at least two key moments: the Great Commission (Jesus' commissioning and sending out of his disciples in Matthew 28.18–20) and Pentecost. At the end of Matthew's Gospel Jesus declares, 'All authority in heaven and on earth has been given to me'; he then says to his disciples:

'Go therefore and make disciples of all nations, baptizing them in the name of the Father and of the Son and of the Holy Spirit, and teaching them to obey everything that I have commanded you. And remember, I am with you always to the end of the age.' (Matt. 28.19–20)

Anglicans are explicitly 'Christocentric' – that is, Jesus Christ is the centre of everything we are and at the centre of everything we do. This is clear from our liturgy; for example, in the so-called 'tri-proclamation' of faith we declare: 'Christ has died, Christ is risen, Christ will come again.' It is also evident in our practice and doctrine; thus, the two sacraments that the Anglican Church recognizes are Holy Baptism and Holy Communion, the sacraments Jesus himself instituted and passed on to his disciples. Christ is at the centre of our *theology* – that is, how we talk and think about God – and also our *ecclesiology* – that is, how we talk and think about the Church.

We are also Trinitarian – baptizing in the name of the Father, the Son and the Holy Spirit just as Jesus instructed. Again, the emphasis on the Holy Trinity is clear in our liturgy; for instance, there are collects that conclude 'Blessed be God, Father, Son and Holy Spirit', and the 'Gloria' is a Trinitarian statement of praise: 'Glory to the Father and to the Son and to the Holy Spirit; as it was in the beginning is now and shall be for ever'. Anglican doctrine also thinks of God in terms of the Holy Trinity; thus Article 1 'Of Faith in the Holy Trinity' of the 39 Articles says the following:

> There is but one living and true God, everlasting, without body, parts, or passions; of infinite power, wisdom, and goodness; the Maker, and Preserver of all things both visible and invisible. And in unity of this Godhead there be three Persons, of one substance, power, and eternity; the Father, the Son, and the Holy Ghost.

Furthermore, early Christianity in the British Isles and Ireland is known to have had a Trinitarian flavour, and in the early fourth century the Celtic Church signed up to the Nicene Creed which sets out key Christian beliefs within a Trinitarian framework. Contemporary expressions of 'Celtic Christianity' have recovered and developed a Trinitarian spirituality, and alternative Anglican liturgies incorporate and develop Trinitarian themes.

As recorded in Matthew's Gospel, Jesus promised to remain with us, and his presence in and among us is attested by the Holy Spirit. Pentecost stands out as a key moment in so far as it signals the beginning of a new era in which the Church – empowered and enabled by the Holy Spirit – gets its teeth into the task that Jesus assigned to it in the Great Commission. This is how Acts 2 begins:

> When the day of Pentecost had come, they were all together in one place. And suddenly from heaven there came a sound

like the rush of a violent wind, and it filled the entire house where they were sitting. Divided tongues, as of fire, appeared among them, and a tongue rested on each of them. All of them were filled with the Holy Spirit and began to speak in other languages, as the Spirit gave them ability. (Acts 2.1–4)

When studying this passage people sometimes focus too much on the phenomenon of spiritual gifts – speaking in tongues – and miss the point of what was actually going on at Pentecost. If we read on into Acts 2, it becomes clear that the miraculous ability to speak in foreign tongues served to point people from all over the world to the good news about the power of God revealed in Jesus (cf. Acts 2.11), a message then solidified in Peter's address. The spiritual empowerment of the apostles at Pentecost enables them to carry out Jesus' call to 'make disciples of all nations'. Again, the encouraging response to the Pentecost preaching and evangelism is couched in terms that tally with Jesus' command to *baptize* new believers and to *teach* them:

> So those who welcomed his [Peter's] message were baptized, and that day about three thousand persons were added. They devoted themselves to the apostles' teaching and fellowship, to the breaking of bread and the prayers. (Acts 2.41–42)

Clearly, at Pentecost the Holy Spirit gave the Church a tremendous kick-start and in that sense it was a unique inaugural 'one-off' occasion. Nevertheless, Anglicans believe that the Holy Spirit continues to energize, equip and refresh God's people in order that we might continue to respond to Christ's call to make disciples of the nations. More 'catholic' Anglicans would point to centuries of Church tradition and growth as the living witness to the work of God's Spirit ministering in and through the Church right up to, and including, the present day. Throughout the Anglican Communion, more charismatic expressions of Anglicanism encourage believers to seek the 'gifts of the Spirit' and to pray for Pentecost-style revivals today.

Can the Holy Spirit work in a 'Pentecost-type way' today? Millions of African Anglicans would reply with an emphatic 'yes' to such a question. Indeed, a good friend of mine and former CMS mission partner shared with me an occasion when he was preaching in an Anglican church in Tanzania. The congregation spoke a local dialect that my friend did not speak, so the church had provided a translator to convert his Swahili sermon into their language. As my friend preached he was surprised that the translator didn't seem to be saying anything, but he just carried on, thinking that the translator might summarize at the end. There was no summary, however. Instead, at the end of the service the bemused translator explained that the words coming out of the missionary's mouth were heard by the church in their local dialect!

To the question 'What are the essentials of Anglican theology?' my answer begins with three characteristic features that are thematic and pop up all over the place in our liturgy and doctrine. First, Anglican theology is *Christ-centred* – Anglicans affirm with the apostle Paul, 'He [Christ] was before all things and in him all things hold together' (Colossians 1.17). Second, Anglican theology is *Trinity-shaped* – Anglicans understand that God is three in one and one in three, Father, Son and Holy Spirit. Third, Anglican theology is *Spirit-fuelled* – Anglicans believe that God's work on earth is made possible by, and in the life-giving power of, the Holy Spirit.

Word and sacrament

Today we have the luxury of carrying the Bible around on our smart phones and tablets, but many Anglican brothers and sisters in developing nations do not enjoy this privilege, nor were the Scriptures so readily available and so accessible in past generations. While the Reformers of the sixteenth century may have had their differences and disagreements on the finer points of theology, they all agreed that reading or preaching from the Vulgate – that is, the Latin translation of the Bible – had very limited use. Since only an elite minority of scholars and nobles could understand Latin, in effect most people were being denied access to the word of God. Article 24 of the 39 Articles makes this point fairly strongly:

> It is a thing plainly repugnant to the Word of God, and the custom of the Primitive Church, to have publick Prayer in the Church, or to minister the Sacraments in a tongue not understanded of the people.

Thus, personally convicted that God speaks in and through the Scriptures, across Europe the Reformers made efforts to translate the Bible into the language spoken by the common people. So it was that the language we now know as German first came to be written down under the influence of Martin Luther. Similarly, to some extent modern English can be traced to the writings of Archbishop Cranmer and his associates who sought to communicate biblical and spiritual truths in words people could understand.

Historically, the Anglican Church has held a 'high view of Scripture'. In other words, far from being a simple book or even a collection of religious writings, the Bible has been treated as a holy book inspired by the Holy Spirit. From the time of the Reformation to the present, the vast majority of Anglicans would take very seriously the claim of 2 Timothy 3.16, 'All Scripture is inspired by God and is useful for teaching, for reproof, for correction, and for training in righteousness.' Article 6 of the 39 Articles identifies the 66 books of the Old and New Testaments as 'canonical' – that is, the *official* books of the Bible 'whose authority was never in any doubt in the Church'.

In the same Article there is a statement that reflects the Reformation idea of *sola Scriptura* – that is, the belief that the testimony of 'Scripture alone' is sufficient for anyone to come to faith in Jesus Christ. Article 6 begins as follows:

> Holy Scripture containeth all things necessary to salvation: so that whatsoever is not read therein, nor may be proved thereby, is not to be required of any man, that it should be believed as an article of the Faith, or be thought requisite or necessary to salvation.

The language might be getting on for 500 years old but the message, I think, remains crystal clear today: there can be no man-made 'bolt-ons' or extra requirements. God has spoken and continues to speak through the living Word, Jesus Christ, and through the written word, the Bible. Scripture, ignited in the heart by the flame of God's Spirit, is the gateway to new and everlasting life in Christ. The mechanics of this are spelt out in Article 11, which explains that salvation comes through Jesus Christ alone and that we are 'justified' by faith in him. As Paul Avis puts it, the theology of the English Reformers offered 'a way of salvation that did not involve the discipline of sacramental penance ... or the pains of purgatory'.[1] In other words, God is the 'Giver of life' and the gift of new life in Christ is offered freely to all with no strings attached. Anglican doctrine shoots down any suggestion that salvation and eternal life can be attained by any moral qualities we might possess or by any 'good works' we might do.

That Scripture continues to be so fundamentally important to Anglicans ought to be obvious from our church services and the tried and tested practice of following the lectionary – the set readings for every day of the year. At every Anglican service of worship some portion of the Bible will be read out loud to the congregation and, if it isn't, something is seriously wrong. It is not unusual to have an Old Testament reading – or, in old language, 'lesson'. But, normally there will also be a New Testament reading and a Gospel reading. As one Brazilian bishop used to joke, 'The preacher might be terrible but since we have so many Bible readings, one way or another the congregation will get the message!'

But it's not just the Bible *readings* that communicate the scriptural message. As explained in the previous chapter, the Anglican liturgy itself draws on and integrates psalms and sentences from the Bible. When we do our confession we turn to the 'penitential psalms' – for example, Psalm 32 and Psalm 51. Sometimes we say or sing great chunks of Scripture such as 'The Benedictus' (The

---

1 Paul Avis, *Anglicanism and the Christian Church*, London: T&T Clark, 2002, p. 7.

Song of Zechariah) or 'The Magnificat' (The Song of Mary). The biblical influence on Anglicanism is apparent on every page of our authorized liturgies and should be obvious in every parish church, irrespective of which particular tradition that church may espouse.

In his 'Prologue or Preface to the Bible' Archbishop Thomas Cranmer epitomized the high view of Scripture that became one of the hallmarks of Anglicanism. Drawing on particular verses he referred to the Bible as 'light', 'food' and 'fire', stating:

the word of God is *light*: your word is a lamp for my feet; *food*: humanity does not live by bread alone, but by all the words of God; *fire*: I have come to send fire on the earth, and how I wish it were already burning![2]

A proper reverence for Scripture is also something that Anglican theologians claimed they had over against what they perceived to be a corrupt Roman Catholic leadership. Thus, John Jewel, Bishop of Salisbury from 1522 to 1571, defends the Church of England, claiming:

We turn the Scriptures into all tongues; they scant suffer them to be had abroad in any tongue. We allure the people to read and to hear God's Word: they drive people from it. We desire to have our cause known to all the world; they flee to come to any trial. We lean unto knowledge, they unto ignorance. We trust unto light, they unto darkness. We reverence, as it becometh us, the writings of the Apostles and the Prophets; and they burnt them.[3]

---

2 Carl S. Meyer, *Cranmer's Selected Writings*, London: SPCK, 1961, 1, but with altered punctuation, emphasis mine and translation mine. In his text, Cranmer gave the Latin of the Bible verses in the citation above, namely: Psalm 119.105, *lucerna pedibus meis verbum tuum*; Luke 4.5, *non in solo pane vivit homo, sed in omni verbo Dei*; and Luke 12.49, *ignem veni mittere in terram, et quid volo, misi ut ardeat?*

3 John Jewel, *The Apology of the Church of England* (Part V), London: Cassell and Company, 1888, p. 139.

Clearly, throughout history, one key way in which the Anglican emphasis on the word of God is felt is through preaching. Bishop Steven Croft states the following:

> The purpose of preaching is to nourish, sustain, inspire, correct and equip the people of God for the mission of God in the world but it is particularly to proclaim the good news of Christ. We are commissioned to tell the story of his birth, life and ministry and especially of his death and resurrection and to call those who listen to repentance, faith and new life.[4]

In today's world where communication is blindingly fast-paced and largely image-based, preachers have to work out *how* best to tell the story of Jesus. Gone are the days when a priest could pontificate for 45 minutes from on high, armed only with a very large Bible and a set of sketchy notes. On the other hand, if the purpose of preaching is indeed 'to nourish, sustain, inspire, correct and equip', then a few PowerPoint slides and a smattering of platitudes and pleasantries really won't do. It is encouraging, then, that in its proposed revised criteria for selection for Ordained Ministry as a Priest, the Church of England intends to require candidates to be 'effective and articulate apologist(s) for Christian faith in the public area', something that presupposes a solid grasp of biblical truths and the ability to communicate these well.[5]

We have seen, then, how the ministry of the word is central to Anglican belief and practice. Equally, in our *Trinity-shaped, Christ-centred* and *Spirit-fuelled* Anglican way of faith and life the ministry of the sacraments is vital. Article 25 of the 39 Articles recognizes Holy Baptism and Holy Communion as sacraments on the basis that Jesus himself commanded his followers to practise these. According to Article 25, the sacraments are 'effectual signs

---

4 Steven Croft, *Ministry in Three Dimensions*, London: Darton, Longman and Todd, 1999, p. 114.

5 Under Criterion F, 'Quality of Mind', in the draft revised Criteria for Selection for Ordained Ministry in the Church of England, expected to be implemented in 2020.

of grace' which 'strengthen' and 'confirm' our faith in God. To paraphrase the classic definition of a 'sacrament', it's an outward visible sign of an internal invisible grace.

Therefore, in regard to Holy Baptism, the water is the outward and visible sign that points to an inner working of God's saving grace in the heart of the believer. The traditional Book of Common Prayer baptism service 'for those of riper years' alludes to Noah, to the Israelites crossing the Red Sea, and to Jesus' own baptism. The baptismal symbolism is fundamentally about dying (drowning) to self and rising to new life in Christ. This sense is captured in what the priest says to the baptized at the conclusion of the Book of Common Prayer service:

> And as for you, who have now by Baptism put on Christ, it is your part and duty also, being made the *children* of God and of the light, by faith in Jesus Christ to walk answerably to your Christian calling, and as becometh the children of light; remembering always that Baptism representeth unto us our profession; which is to follow the example of our Saviour Christ, and to be made like unto him; that as he died, and rose again for us, so should we who are baptized, die from sin and rise again unto righteousness.

Again, since water is used to clean our bodies in washing, Holy Baptism also communicates the sense in which our hearts are cleansed by the purifying influence of Jesus as he comes into our lives. The early Christian movement documented in the book of Acts lays great emphasis on the baptism of new believers. Great crowds of people are baptized (e.g. Acts 2.41), whole households are baptized (e.g. Acts 16.33), and so are individual converts (e.g. Acts 8.36–38). Baptism is symbolic of a new start and a new way of life for the follower of Christ.

A couple of questions always come up whenever baptism is mentioned. The first is a 'who' question and concerns *who* ought to be baptized – in particular, whether children and babies should be baptized. For centuries, the practice of nearly every wing of

Christianity has been to baptize infants as well as adults and this is standard in the Anglican Communion. In the early Christian period key figures such as Saint Augustine claimed that infant baptism had always been practised in the Church.

Anglicans understand that in the case of infants, baptism is the act by which a person is welcomed into the embrace of the Church. It is about *belonging*, and analogy is often made to circumcision that was an 'outward sign' showing that the Jewish boy belonged to the people of God. In infant baptism, parents and godparents commit to bringing up the child in the Christian faith and to pray for them. In time, as the person takes ownership of the promises prayed over them at baptism, their faith is *confirmed* and publicly affirmed in the service of 'confirmation', where a bishop prays for them.

The second question that is usually tacked on to discussions around baptism is the *how* question – in particular, should baptism be by 'full immersion' or can it be by 'aspersion'? In short, does it have to be a total dunking or will a sprinkling do? It's a sad fact that historically this question about method has caused such tortuous divisions between Christians. Ultimately, if the sacrament is really about the inner working of God's grace in the heart it shouldn't matter which form the outward 'sign' takes. I have been involved in highly moving adult baptisms done in tropical rivers, and even on Brazilian beaches. Equally, though, on profoundly spiritual and joyful occasions I have sprinkled water and signed the cross on the forehead of babies presented by prayerful and deeply committed Christian families in parish churches.

As we have discussed in relation to other matters, similarly with Holy Baptism the Anglican approach seeks to be *inclusive* rather than *exclusive*. The commitment of Anglicanism to unity in diversity allows for a variety of forms but without compromise in regard to the central truth to which the sacrament bears witness. Whether it's an adult sinking beneath the surface of the local swimming pool or a sprinkled baby, the message from the Church is 'welcome' and 'we commit to walking with you and praying for you on your faith journey'.

If Holy Baptism is essentially a one-off 'initiation rite', then the sacrament that signals belonging and being named among the people of God – Holy Communion or Eucharist – might be seen as a 'continuation rite', the sacrament that on a regular and ongoing basis reminds us who we belong to and who we are in Christ. The nineteenth-century German theologian Schleiermacher used to describe sin as 'forgetfulness' – forgetting God and who we truly are as a people who have been given a brand-new identity in Jesus. Taking Holy Communion regularly helps us confront our habitual forgetfulness, reminding us of who we truly are by refocusing and reinforcing our identity in Christ.[6]

In the first place, as the etymology of the word 'Eucharist' implies, this 'meal' is a thanksgiving celebration of what God did for us through Jesus. It is a thanksgiving for Jesus' saving death and an expression of gratitude for the new life we have in Christ through his resurrection. The words of the liturgy, 'feed on him by faith', indicate that this event strengthens and feeds those who have given their lives to Christ. Nevertheless, Anglicans from the time of the Reformers in the sixteenth century have realized that there is an element of 'mystery' to what happens at Holy Communion. In a sense that words struggle to explain, Jesus becomes intimately and personally present to the sincere believer who 'takes and eats' and who 'drinks the cup'.

The outward symbolic elements are the bread and wine, though by extension the vestments and instruments that adorn the Holy Table have symbolic significance. The inward action of God's grace has several dimensions that can be summed up in the language of *encounter*. For me, this notion of *encounter* with the crucified and risen Christ is helpful since it encompasses the

---

6 For a brief introduction to Eucharistic services/theology, see Mark Beach, *Using Common Worship Holy Communion: A Practical Guide to the New Services*. London: Church House Publishing, 2000.

temporal, the spatial, the personal and the collective aspects of Holy Communion.

Unpacking this a little, the temporal aspect of the Eucharistic *encounter* focuses on the present moment when, by symbolically receiving Jesus' 'body and blood', we invite him to meet with us in the deepest recesses of our heart and being. The *encounter* happens in the 'here and now' of receiving Communion, but is anchored also in the 'back then' of Calvary. As the ancient liturgy explains, building on Jesus' instruction 'do this in remembrance of me', Holy Communion is a 'memorial', a poignant reminder and recollection of Jesus' sacrifice 'made once for all' in times past. Since the sacrament also looks forward to our ultimate union with Christ in the fullness of time, there is very much a future 'still to come' angle to it too. Theologians speak of the 'messianic banquet', a picture of *shalom* prosperity and peace where God's people enjoy Holy Table fellowship with Jesus in eternity.

Temporally, then, the special encounter with Jesus in the 'now' of Holy Communion recalls the 'once for all' sacrifice that happened 'back then', while also looking forward with joyful expectation to the resurrection life that is 'still to come'. The spatial aspect recognizes that the physical place in which the believer receives the sacrament and so encounters Jesus becomes a 'sacred space'. More importantly, as we 'feed on him by faith' there is a sense in which the body as 'temple of the Holy Spirit' becomes the sanctified space in which God's grace is operative. In gratitude, remembering that Jesus offered his life for us, by partaking in this sacrament we offer our souls and bodies to his service, asking him to come into our disordered lives and to make us whole.

Very often people find it difficult to articulate *what* exactly is going on during Holy Communion, and again this is partly because words struggle to convey what is a deeply spiritual moment and event. Nevertheless, when asked to describe what this sacrament is all about, invariably people speak of how *personal* this meeting with Jesus is. The personal dimension of Holy Communion recognizes that each human being was created in the image and likeness of God. Sin and wrongdoing distorts this image and takes us on a path that leads away from God towards brokenness, chaos, emptiness and death. Through Jesus' sacrifice the individual believer is restored and reshaped so that he or she may once again reflect God's goodness and love.

There is, therefore, a sense in which Holy Communion pulls together the unique threads of one's personal journey. The twists and turns of our personal stories are brought to Jesus as we offer ourselves to his service, asking that he lead us forward for the remainder of the journey. Most Eucharistic liturgies refer directly or indirectly to the 'way of the cross' in reference to the life of discipleship that the Christian commits to when taking Communion. Thus, in Prayer B of the Common Worship Series' Eucharistic prayers, mention is made of Jesus' death on the cross and the prayer reaches a crescendo with the words: 'we thank you for counting us worthy to stand in your presence and serve you'.[7] Just as Jesus put God and others first, coming 'not to be served but to serve' (Mark 10.45), so each one of us must follow Christ's self-giving example of loving service in our day-to-day lives.

Given the strength of the personal experience of encounter with Jesus that communicants acknowledge, it would be easy to skate over the *collective* aspect of Holy Communion. I often use the form of the cross to explain how Jesus' death reconciles us to God vertically, as it were, but also to each other, as it were, horizontally. The Anglican confessional liturgy is a great leveller – in the Church of England, monarch and servant alike bow before God as one. Together, in the liturgy, we recognize our individual and corporate errors and shortcomings. Preparing for Communion in prayer, as the family of faith we 'confess our sins before Almighty God' and we also seek to be reconciled to one another. Thus, 'The Peace' is an essential moment of the Eucharistic liturgy and more than an opportunity to shake a couple of hands or pat someone

7 See Mark Beach, *Using Common Worship Holy Communion: A Practical Guide to the New Services*. London: Church House Publishing, 2000, p. 74.

on the back; it's the time to 'get right' before God with the person we've fallen out with.

Just as the Jewish Passover meal recalls and re-tells the Exodus story of a people journeying with God from slavery to liberty, so Holy Communion connects with the larger narrative of God intervening in history to save his people. As the Passover Lamb was sacrificed in the place of the firstborn son of the Hebrews, so Jesus, 'the Lamb who takes away the sin of the world', died in our place. Around the Holy Table we congregate as people of the 'new covenant', through Jesus' death and resurrection, and God's promises of liberty, love and life extend to us as *new* Israel. Each of us has his or her individual faith journey, but as the family of faith we journey together on the road of healing, mercy, love and life.

Beyond the temporal, spatial, personal and collective dimensions of the encounter with Christ in the Eucharist, there are many other nuances reflected in our Anglican liturgies. The 'mechanics' of salvation are spelt out in the Eucharistic prayers. Thus, there are references to the cleansing and purifying effect that Jesus' blood has on our lives, how he rescues us from death, bringing forgiveness of sins and the promise of new life. Other emphases include thanksgiving for creation, where bread and wine are identified as physical gifts of God's creation, and sometimes as signs of plenitude that point in the direction of the new heavens and the new earth. It's fair to say that in relation to Holy Communion or the Eucharist, our Anglican theology and liturgy reaches its lyrical and spiritual best.

Scripture, tradition and reason

In discussions on Anglican theology, it's never long before someone mentions the 'three-legged stool' of Scripture, tradition and reason, attributing this categorization to the sixteenth-century theologian Richard Hooker. Technically, in his *Laws of Ecclesiastical Polity*, on the rare occasion that Hooker spoke of

these three, he did so in terms of sources of the Church's authority rather than as a basis for theology. Again, for the record,
Hooker wrote about Scripture, reason and tradition ('the voice
of the Church') in that order.

Nowadays when theologians talk about 'Scripture, tradition and
reason' the idea is that Anglicanism '*does* theology' and reaches
conclusions about its very essence and life by appealing to these
three sources. While the 'stool' image gives the impression of a
balanced approach, and while some contemporary Anglican
thinkers might choose to put these categories on an equal footing,
possibly throwing in 'experience' to make it a four-legged stool,
Hooker's own writings suggest he regarded Scripture as the highest source of authority.[8] This, in fact, is consistent with the view
put forward in the 39 Articles. Thus, Article 20 of the 39 Articles
concerns the authority of the Church, but delimits this according
to a biblical framework when it stipulates: 'it is not lawful for
the Church to ordain any thing that is contrary to God's Word
written ...'

On closer examination it emerges that, historically, Anglican
thinking about the authority of the Church, and indeed theology, presupposes the primacy of Scripture. Our God-given
human intelligence ('reason') and the pronouncements/creeds/
rulings of the Church ('tradition') are not so much separate
sources as secondary witnesses, which complement and support
the authority, teaching and testimony of Scripture. Today, in
the 85 million-member Anglican Communion, the vast majority
of Anglicans would agree that it is through the Bible that God
makes himself known to us, and as '*Holy* Scripture' it remains
our highest source of authority.

---

8 Richard Hooker, *Laws of Ecclesiastical Polity.* V. 8.2, Oxford: Clarendon
Press, 1876, pp. 33–34.

So, summing up, what are the essentials of Anglican theology?

In this chapter we have seen how Anglican theology is Christ-centred, Trinity-shaped and Spirit-fuelled. Picking up on points made in earlier chapters, we have established that Anglican theology places a dual emphasis on the importance of the word – that is, the Bible – and the importance of sacraments – that is, Holy Baptism and Holy Communion. In discussions of Anglican theology or the methodology used in Anglicanism the so-called 'three-legged stool' of Scripture, tradition and reason is frequently alluded to. While Anglican theology does draw on all three, historically Scripture has been regarded as the highest source of authority for Anglicans, and that continues to be the case for the vast majority of Anglicans in the worldwide Anglican Communion.

Questions for individual or group reflection

1 In what ways is Anglican theology rooted in the Bible?
2 Reflect a little on your experience of Anglican churches. Where have you encountered a strongly Christ-centred approach? Can you think of a particular church or place where a Trinitarian focus has been evident? In which churches has the life, vision and mission been clearly Spirit-fuelled?
3 What is a 'high view of Scripture' and how is it clear that Anglicanism has a 'high view of Scripture'?
4 Why is Holy Baptism important for Anglicans, and how do Anglicans understand infant baptism?
5 How important is taking Holy Communion to you, and what have you learnt about it in this chapter?

5

What happens when
Anglicans disagree?

Though preachers sometimes present the Church in Acts as if it were free from problems, the biblical text itself suggests otherwise. In point of fact, there were significant disagreements between groups (e.g. Acts 15.2), and significant disagreements between key leaders (e.g. Acts 15.39). If, in the earliest days of the Church there were differences of opinion, it shouldn't surprise us that Christians, including Anglicans, still can and do disagree. We are, after all, only human.

Over the years, Anglicans have disagreed on all kinds of things – for example, from which direction the altar should face, to the legitimacy or otherwise of slavery and, in some African contexts, polygamy. As in the Church in Acts, disagreements can arise between key leaders; for example, in the eighteenth-century evangelical revival, George Whitefield and John Wesley shared many values, but Whitefield was a convinced Calvinist, and Wesley an ardent Arminian. (Calvinists stress predestination and salvation by God's grace without the participation of the human will; Arminians stress the co-operation of the human will with the grace of God in the act of a person's individual salvation.) In general, both Whitefield and Wesley fell out with diocesan bishops they came into contact with, largely because they were unwilling to restrict their preaching to parish boundaries.

Within Anglicanism, disagreements often arise between groups. Thus, from the reign of Elizabeth I, Puritans and 'Prayer Book Anglicans' fell out about all manner of matters, theological and spiritual. In the early years of the twentieth century, the Anglican mission organization CMS experienced internal turbulence that led, ultimately, to the creation of a second organization – BCMS (Bible Churchmen's Missionary Society). And in the twenty-first century Anglicanism/Episcopalianism in North America has divided over the issue of sexuality and the Church.

Among the issues over which Anglicans have disagreed in recent decades is women's ordination. This was not simply an argument about equality. Biblical arguments for and against it were put forward by opposing sides, while Anglo-Catholics made the point that as part of the 'one, holy, catholic and apostolic Church', no such change could be made without damaging relationships with the Orthodox and Roman Catholic Churches that do not ordain women. Today, women priests and bishops are found in many parts of the Anglican Communion, although the Church of England has provided for those parishes who cannot, in all conscience, accept this change with 'flying bishops' who minister to such parishes. While the majority of parishes and people are in favour of women's ordination, others remain opposed on biblical grounds. The road travelled by the Anglican Communion on this issue has been a long and at times tortuous one, nor is this particular journey over: tensions can and do still flare up, and there is more work to be done. Neither should we pass over the fact that both men and women carry scars and hurts from these debates that are very real. Nevertheless, as a worldwide Church, we seem to be learning how to agree to disagree on this, to live and let live with our differences in Christ.

Seemingly, though, disagreements over homosexuality pose a more serious threat to the unity of the Anglican Church. Given that Anglicans have managed to live with their differences on other contentious matters, it seems reasonable to ask, 'Can't we just agree to disagree on this one too?' But that, of course, is exactly what the Anglican Communion has been unable to do – so far at least. Arguably, no other topic has rocked the Anglican foundations in quite the same way. On the other hand, some commentators draw attention to the fact that in the past

Anglican Churches disagreed over slavery, the remarriage of divorcees, and also the role of women in ministry, but despite apparently insuperable differences the Church is still here, change has happened, and life goes on.[1] One way or another, it has been possible to move forward as a Church, in spite of some very real and painful disagreements.

On some divisive topics, as in the historic case of slavery, there has been a real sea change, a complete rethink of prevailing attitudes in society and within Anglicanism. More recently, on other divisive issues such as the remarrying of divorcees, a respectful distance and commitment to mutual flourishing has been the outcome. Tensions can and do play a part in church life, and Anglicans have been able to put aside their differences on all sorts of things so as to work together for the greater good, and indeed the common good. So again we might ask, should things be any different in relation to homosexuality?

Whether or not we think that things *should* be any different, the fact is *they are*. This is indicated by the major institutional challenges now faced by the Anglican Communion (cf. Chapter 8 on the Anglican Communion), not least the existence of multinational Anglican movements such as GAFCON that have arisen as a direct response to this sole issue. The structures of Anglicanism are stretched and vexed by this question on a scale that is beyond anything we have experienced previously.

In the light of the weightiness of the challenge, some characterizations of what is currently playing out in the Anglican Communion aren't very helpful. It will not do, for instance, to frame the question of homosexuality within Anglicanism as the struggle between post-colonial nations and the developed West.[2] This type of simplification is likely to be seen as patronizing by bishops and theologians of 'post-colonial' nations. Moreover, it

---

1 For example, Martyn Percy, *The Future Shapes of Anglicanism: Currents, Contours, Charts.* London: Routledge, 2017, p. 129.

2 This appears to be how the matter is framed, for example, in Mark Chapman, *Anglican Theology*, London: T&T Clark, 2012, pp. 199–201.

downplays the concrete reality that there are articulate voices on both sides of the fence in all quarters – for instance, you'll find 'traditionalists' in the UK and North America, and 'revisionists' in 'post-colonial' contexts in South America and South Africa.

Asking the right questions

Where the unity of the Church is threatened, it's very important to formulate the right questions and to avoid knee-jerk answers. To start with, we might ask:

> Are there systems that can enable the Anglican Communion or Church of England to negotiate intense disagreements, or navigate through complex arguments? Is it possible to find consensus in the midst of heated debates and a distancing in relations?[3]

These are the right sort of questions, and if any 'consensus' is to be found on the trickiest of problems, we have to begin – to paraphrase Tom Wright – by differentiating between the differences between us that make a *real difference* and those that make *little difference*.[4] Facing the present challenges, the realization that we have certain key beliefs and values in common with those with whom we disagree – something that at first might be difficult to recognize – may help to put a brake on further 'distancing in relations'. At the risk of stating the obvious, taking the time to listen properly to those we disagree with and taking the trouble to get to know them as human beings is the first step to 'establish and maintain holy friendship'.[5]

---

3 Martyn Percy, *Anglicanism: Confidence, Commitment and Communion*, Farnham: Ashgate, 2013, p. 15.

4 Tom Wright, 'Pastoral Theology for Perplexing Topics: Paul and Adiaphora' (pp. 63–82), in A. Atherstone and A. Goddard (eds), *Good Disagreement? Grace and Truth in a Divided Church*, London: Lion, 2015, p. 67.

5 The phrase is that of my friend Elizabeth Stuart, sourced from 'Dancing in the Spirit' (pp. 71–85), in Timothy Bradshaw (ed.), *The Way Forward? Christian Voices on Homosexuality and the Church*, London: SCM Press, 2003, p. 84.

Historically, in Anglicanism, the rationale summed up by Tom Wright has been fundamental to working out our differences in church tradition and spirituality. Emerging from the turbulent tug-of-war years of Reformation and post-Reformation Europe, over time Anglican theologians shaped the Church of England so as to accommodate both Reformed and Catholic emphases. With the importance of Scripture and the historic creeds as, so to speak, the lowest common denominator, for centuries Anglicans have learned to live with one another and to live with their differences.[6]

True, disagreements have sometimes been sharp, and at times the possibility of 'meeting in the middle' or 'agreeing to disagree' has looked remote. For example, the 'high church' revival in Victorian England was deeply troubling to Anglican evangelical spirituality, and vice versa. From a twenty-first-century English perspective, where a parish church can offer traditional and con-temporary services back to back on a Sunday morning, it would be easy to underestimate just how intense these disagreements were in the nineteenth century. Over time, though, something has shifted. Evangelicals and Anglo-Catholics may still regard one another with a degree of suspicion, but nine times out of ten clergy are committed to working together in partnership, and divisions along 'party' lines are nothing like the problem they once were.

It is possible, then, to come from very different places, spiritually and theologically, while remaining part of the same Church and recognizing one another as part of the same family of faith. Over the years, the Anglican principle of 'comprehensiveness' has allowed for what I would call 'generous disagreement' in regard to many matters. Indeed, the development of worldwide Anglicanism and the global Anglican Communion has, at its

---

6 Of course, there have been those who have felt unable to do this and have jumped ship – for example, Puritans such as Richard Baxter reluctantly departed from the Church of England because in their view it wasn't *Reformed* enough, whereas John Henry Newman and other champions of the Oxford Movement transferred to the Roman Catholic Church because in their view the Church of England wasn't *Catholic* enough.

heart, a simultaneous recognition of that which unites us, and those things that distinguish us. Anglicanism has long seen value in the maxim: 'unity in the essential things, freedom in the uncertain things, and charity in everything'.[7]

But how about the difficulty in discerning what the *essential things* are? This, arguably, is where debates over sexuality pose more of a challenge than those that Anglicanism has faced to date. For example, however significant, few Anglicans ever considered women's ministry a 'first order' issue.[8] By contrast, it is important to comprehend that the majority of global Anglicans regard human sexuality as an *essential* or 'first order' issue. In other words, it is held that one's sexual practice can affect one's salvation and spiritual well-being. On this view, homosexual practice is judged to be incompatible with the Christian faith – which view, in turn, appears unpalatable and incomprehensible to Christians who pursue the 'full inclusion' of homosexuals in the Anglican Church. Thus, on the face of it, within global Anglicanism it is proving difficult to come to 'good disagreement' on this matter. Moreover, in parts of the Anglican Communion, de facto disagreements on the ground have not been 'good' (cf. Chapter 8).

Room for manoeuvre?

When Anglicanism finds itself racked by tensions over challenging issues, theologians appeal to Scripture, tradition and reason – sometimes throwing in experience – in attempts to break the stalemate. Alan Suggate says the following in relation to the trusty trio of Scripture, tradition and reason:

---

7 Ironically, it was Richard Baxter – who, albeit reluctantly, left the Church of England – who was responsible for popularizing this maxim in English.

8 In the Church of England, a small percentage of clergy and laity have left the Church over this issue in recent decades, and some have been welcomed into the Roman Catholic Church. Even then, I am not convinced that all those who opted to leave would say that this was a de facto 'first order' issue, if by 'first order' we mean that which has a direct effect on one's salvation.

The supreme criterion for the Christian life is the revelation of God in Christ, of which Scripture is the inspired record. Tradition is also vital. One could not come to faith except through the tradition embodied in the Church. Yet there is no safety in simply handing it down. Tradition is also the experience of Christians living adventurously in response to those revelatory events ... This involves the exercise of reason – for example, a grasp of science and how it relates to faith, and a continual dialogue with philosophers and indeed with all those seeking to understand and shape life in its various facets.[9]

At times, this 'living adventurously' referred to above has involved questioning and even overturning traditions handed down, by returning to the 'revelatory events' enshrined in Scripture and reasoning things through afresh. After all, as Saint Cyprian put it, 'tradition without truth is simply error grown old'.[10] Over 200 years ago, in the Church of England, even prominent evangelical reformers such as George Whitefield pointed to passages of Scripture that attested to the practice of slavery in order to argue for its legitimacy. It took a combination of careful biblical interpretation, arguments from tradition and experience to demonstrate the incompatibility of slavery with Christianity.[11] Eventually this resulted in a total change of attitude and a revolutionary reframing of the question.

Anglican opinions may still be divided on women's ordination, but my experience in four continents bears witness to a growing appetite for 'good disagreement'. By 'good disagreement' I mean that individuals are able to agree to disagree, remaining in partnership in the work of the gospel, recognizing and respecting one another's different viewpoints – and indeed one another – as

---

9 Alan M. Suggate, 'The Temple Tradition', in Malcolm Brown (ed.), *Anglican Social Theology*, London: Church House Publishing, 2014, pp. 29–30.

10 Sourced from John Barton, 'Why Not Have Women Bishops? Meeting the Challenge Head-on' (pp. 13–24), in Harriet Harris and Jane Shaw (eds), *The Call for Women Bishops*, London: SPCK, 2004, p. 20.

11 Interestingly, this is another issue on which Wesley and Whitefield disagreed, with Wesley eventually writing an anti-slavery piece.

members of the same family of faith. Even if they themselves are unpersuaded, in conversation those against women's ordination usually concede that opponents make positive appeals to Scripture – pointing out, for example, Jesus' radical inclusion of women and references to women leaders in Paul's letters. Most find that women in ministry is a 'secondary' issue and are content to sign up to 'mutual flourishing' in the interests of the gospel.

Is there any room for manoeuvre on present controversies surrounding homosexuality and the Church then, and might appeals to Scripture, tradition, reason and experience somehow unpick the deadlock? The jury is still out on that one, and the most we can hope to do is sketch some of the complexities of the disagreement and appeal for wise and warm words from both sides of the divide.

First of all, on both sides of the fence there are characteristic problems in approach. On social media – and sometimes in serious debate – some who appeal to Scripture in support of a traditional view on human sexuality can be prone to 'prooftexting' – that is, quoting isolated verses in a reductionist fashion without taking into account broader considerations.[12] Apart from anything else, 'the letter' of some biblical teaching was clearly intended for an ancient people in an Ancient Near Eastern culture, and has little direct relevance for us today. Thus if, so to speak, a coherent 'no' is to be given to the question of homosexuality and the Church, then a more discerning handling of the Scriptures is needed, properly accounting for the overarching narrative of salvation and the fullness of God's revelation in Christ.[13]

Conversely, Anglicans who favour 'full inclusion' sometimes appear too keen to align the homosexuality debate with other

---

12 On this danger, see Carolyn Sharp's 'Beyond Prooftexting', in Andrew Linzey and Richard Kirker (eds), *Gays and the Future of Anglicanism: Responses to the Windsor Report*, Winchester: O Books, 2005, pp. 30–49.

13 Similarly, Oliver O'Donovan, in Timothy Bradshaw (ed.), *The Way Forward? Christian Voices on Homosexuality and the Church*, London: SCM Press, 2003, p. 28.

debates, such as the slavery debate.[14] There may be certain similarities between the two, but in terms of questions over Scripture there is a difference. Whereas abolitionists successfully argued that the entire sweep of Scripture is pro-freedom and opposed to slavery (from the Exodus liberation narrative to the notion of 'redemption' and freedom in Christ from the 'slavery of sin'), on the face of it Scripture contains only 'uncompromisingly negative references' to homosexual practice. Certainly, these texts must be seen within a broader framework and there is a bigger picture to be discerned. Nevertheless, if a coherent 'yes' is to be given to the question of homosexuality and the Church, these texts do 'demand an account'.[15]

Naturally, Scripture does not exist in a vacuum, and Anglicans bring experiential factors to bear on the question of homosexuality and biblical interpretation. But individuals' experience is as diverse and complex as the different arguments for and against 'full inclusion' put forward in Anglican synods and Lambeth Conferences. Thus, if in current debates it is right to hear gay Christians who experience and practise their sexuality positively as a *gift*, is it therefore wrong to allow a voice to gay Christians who experience their sexuality as a *burden* and opt to remain celibate? The Church needs to take seriously the experience of gay Christians who have been in faithful and flourishing same-sex relationships for years, but it also needs to take seriously the experience of Christians who once identified as gay but are now married to partners of the opposite sex, or those who are celibate, believing that the Holy Spirit enables them to live fulfilled lives in holiness and fellowship as celibate gay people.

---

14 Martyn Percy, *The Shapes of Anglicanism: Currents, Contours, Charts*, London: Routledge, 2017, pp. 91–2.

15 The quotation and the one in the previous sentence are drawn from Oliver O'Donovan, 'Homosexuality in the Church: Can There Be a Fruitful Theological Debate?' (pp. 20–36), in Timothy Bradshaw (ed.), *The Way Forward? Christian Voices on Homosexuality and the Church*, London: SCM Press, 2003, p. 28.

The difficulty here, of course, lies in competing narratives and the inherent problems bound up with subjective experience. But if experiential factors and the questions they pose weren't enough of a headache, cultural considerations can further muddy the waters. Thus, horror stories of gay people being subjected to exorcisms or coerced into undergoing medical treatments in order to 'cure' them of their homosexuality seem abhorrent and inadmissible to the vast majority of us who live in the cultural climate of the UK or USA today. However, many African Anglicans find it abhorrent and inadmissible that same-sex relationships might be considered 'normal', believing homosexuality to be a condition or state from which people need to be 'delivered'. Moreover, they argue that a 'liberal' approach to human sexuality damages their credibility when in dialogue with other faiths, such as Islam, that hold a strongly conservative line on these matters. I remember commenting to a Kenyan friend how I found it troubling and difficult to believe that in England not so long ago people went to prison for being practising homosexuals. He replied that he found it difficult to believe that people in England *no longer* go to prison for being practising homosexuals. That Christians are nowhere near 'on the same page' on this issue is plain to see.

To reiterate something from earlier on, on this controversial theme there's a real danger that in thrashing out our ideas we end up thrashing each other and things can get painfully personal. Agreeing or disagreeing with one another, we should all consider that we are loved, accepted and, in the area of our sexuality, challenged and saved by Jesus.

So, what happens when Anglicans disagree?

'Good disagreement', I would suggest, is part of the Anglican ethos and identity, and in the Anglican Communion it would seem to link back to the concept of 'comprehensiveness'. On all manner of divisive issues, Anglicans have been able to agree to disagree, because the essential principle of unity on 'first order'/ 'essential' matters has been retained. While accepting that there are still challenges, I have opined that this is the emerging picture in the Anglican Communion in relation to women's ordination.

On the specific dilemma of homosexuality and the Church, things are extra tricky since, in Anglicanism, the global majority hold a traditional view, considering this to be an essential, 'first order' issue over which there can be no compromise, whereas a minority aligned with powerful majority secular voices believe that 'full inclusion' is similarly *essential*. Some merely hope for a future in which it will be possible to 'agree to disagree' on homosexuality. On both sides, though, there are those who maintain that this matter is non-negotiable, that 'agreeing to disagree' on homosexuality is simply unthinkable.

Anglican history teaches us that many disagreements can be overcome by appealing to Scripture, tradition and reason, and working out a way forward together. This may or may not be possible in the current climate, with some aspiring to 'good disagreement' and others consciously 'walking apart'. One thing is clear to me, though: far from dehumanizing those whose views we find strange, offensive and unpalatable, against all the odds 'holy friendship' can be a real possibility. Such friendship, I'm sure, must be allowed to flourish, even if that means finding new ways of disagreeing.

Questions for individual or group reflection

1 Why does the 'Anglican ethos' encourage us to pursue 'good disagreement', and where have you personally seen 'good disagreement' on the ground?
2 How do you think that in terms of divisive issues in the Anglican Communion, decisions made in one Province – for example, the Church of England, the Episcopal Church in the USA or one of the African Churches – have an impact on other Anglican Churches?

3 What is your own perspective on Christianity and homosexuality, and why is it that you think as you do on this
question? How would you relate to someone who holds a different view?
4 Reflect on the different Anglican views on women's ministry.
Can you understand why those who think differently to you
believe what they believe?
5 Is it possible for Anglicans who hold radically different views
on issues relating to the ordination of women and/or human
sexuality to remain 'in communion' and in mission together? If
so, *how*?

6

How do Anglicans understand
vocation and calling?

One of the key emphases of the Reformation was its insistence that Christian vocation starts at baptism, not ordination. In other words, you don't need a dog collar to make a difference for Jesus. Instead, every single follower of Christ is called to play a part in the life of the Church and the mission of God in the world. This ought to be clear from the famous body metaphor that Paul uses when explaining to the Christians in Corinth that every person matters. Is one body part more valuable than another? No, you need all of them if the body is to function well! Moreover, Paul warns those tempted to think of themselves as spiritually superior to others that the apparently less valuable bits of the body should be honoured and cared for (cf. 1 Corinthians 12.12–31).

Anglicanism takes this New Testament teaching seriously and advocates the idea that the whole people of God are called to live for Christ in the world. This is borne out by the fact that, both nationally and locally, Anglican Churches are led by dedicated groups of normal church folk who partner with clergy in church governance. Synods are gatherings of lay and ordained representatives who meet to pray, discuss and take decisions on important matters in the life of the Church. Thus 'General Synod' in England, Australia and Canada, and 'General Convention' in the USA, refers to the national gathering of leaders, both lay and ordained.

Locally, the responsibility for the running of the parish church is also a joint effort, bringing together ordained ministers and lay members. Anglican Churches around the world have their equivalent of what the Church of England calls the PCC – Parochial Parish Council. Amusingly, in Brazil the initials PCC are associated with an organized crime faction, so the equivalent shorthand is JP instead! The PCC is a prime example of Anglicanism's commitment to Christian vocation as a partnership between ordained and lay people. Membership of lay people is determined on a rolling system, so different individuals get the chance to join the team for a set term (normally three years):

> 'PCC' stands for 'Parochial Church Council'. It is a legal body, made up of the people who have legal responsibility for the … parish church, the churchyard, and the church's money. Importantly, though, the PCC also has responsibility for working with the minister on matters of general concern and importance to the parish, and promoting the whole mission of the Church in the parish. It works for all in its parish, not just on running the church building or looking after the Christians.[1]

The vision that we all have a part to play in God's mission is also explicit in our church services. The liturgy is by definition inclusive, inviting the gathered congregation to make responses and join in with prayers and worship. Again, the final words of Anglican services often act as a reminder that our faith doesn't hibernate during the week, only to be wheeled out on Sundays. In England the minister says, 'Go in peace to love and serve the Lord,' and the congregation replies, 'In the name of Christ, Amen!' At the end of Anglican services in Brazil the congregation say together: 'Let's go in the peace of Christ, let's be courageous and strong in the witness of the gospel among all people and let's serve the Lord with gladness – Alleluia!' In true Brazilian style, a fist pump accompanies the loud 'Alleluia!'

---

1 Mark Tanner, *The PCC Member's Essential Guide*, London: Church House Publishing, 2015, p. 6.

Thus, in the widest sense of the word, Anglicanism understands that 'vocation' is all about being a true disciple of Jesus in our day-to-day lives. As Canon Christina Baxter once remarked, 'You can't have a day off from being a Christian!'[2] On the contrary, as the people of God, our lives are to point to the reality of his love 24/7. This is as true of the child at school as it is of the great-grandparent in the care home. It goes for the parish priest zipping about his or her 'patch', but equally it goes for every member of the congregation – from the 16-year-old stacking shelves to the silver-haired barrister in the court room.

Dietrich Bonhoeffer reminds us in his reflections on the Sermon on the Mount that true discipleship requires both a visible public presence and an invisible private devotion.[3] The 'public' bit is what we mentioned above, sharing Jesus by living transparently as Christians each day. Privately, our commitment will be about opening our hearts to God in quiet reflection. It will be about refusing to be overcome by evil and overcoming evil with good (cf. Romans 12.21). In the terms of the Sermon on the Mount, it will be about kicking bad life-draining habits and adopting good life-giving patterns, as we learn to pray more regularly, fast more zealously, and give more generously.

True discipleship means standing up and being counted for Christ. For many Anglicans around the world responding to Christ's call can be a risky business. During my time in Brazil our diocese was linked to a so-called companion diocese in northern Nigeria. I forget the number of times we were asked to pray for the faithful bishop and people of that place as time and again they were beaten, and their homes and church buildings burned down by Islamic extremists. Recently, I visited the Parish of the Martyrs in Uige, Angola, where in the 1960s a group of Anglican ministers were executed by Portuguese soldiers in the war of

---

2 At a pre-ordination retreat for the Diocese of Winchester, held at Park Place, Wickham on 30 June 2017.

3 Dietrich Bonhoeffer, *The Cost of Discipleship*, London: SCM Press, 1996, pp. 141–2.

independence. In a similar vein, the Church of England diocese of which I am now a part is twinned with (among others) the Province of Myanmar, another place where Christians are frequently subjected to violence and repression.

It is said that the number of Christians killed for their faith in the twentieth century is more than the sum of those martyred in all the other centuries put together, and the Anglican Communion continues to live with this reality. For those fortunate enough to live in stable societies in developed nations this sobering news ought to stir us to value our freedom and spur us into getting serious about our calling. Sometimes we need a bit of a spiritual reality check to shake us out of complacency and reignite our vocation. Praying for persecuted brothers and sisters in the Anglican Communion provides support for them and focus for us as we reaffirm our own calling to follow Jesus and make the most of the freedoms we enjoy.

Whereas our struggles in the UK are rarely about life-threatening persecution, that doesn't mean they are insignificant. Daily, Jesus calls us to die to self and to choose to live for him. As we learn to let go of our egocentric agendas, we must ask God's Spirit to reshape our priorities and refashion our thinking. In our daily lives, then, Jesus calls each and every one of us – ordained and lay – to kick our innate selfishness into touch in order to follow him in the narrow way of self-sacrificial love and action.

One way of understanding our common Christian calling is to think in terms of Jesus' two 'greats' – the Great Commandment and the Great Commission:

> [Jesus said] '"You shall love the Lord your God with all your heart, and with all your soul, and with all your mind." This is the greatest and first commandment. And a second is like it: "You shall love your neighbour as yourself." On these two commandments hang all the law and the prophets.' (Matthew 22.37–40)

[Jesus said] 'Go therefore and make disciples of all nations, baptizing them in the name of the Father and of the Son and of the Holy Spirit, and teaching them to obey everything that I have commanded you. And remember, I am with you always, to the end of the age.' (Matthew 28.19–20)

While some might want to apply the Great Commandment as a kind of rule of life for lay disciples and the Great Commission as a mandate exclusively for clergy, this would be a mistake. It's true that ordained ministers have a special responsibility to baptize, to teach the faith, and to make new disciples but they don't do this in holy hermit-style isolation. Rather, the entire Church ought to be involved in these life-giving actions, be it sharing Jesus with work colleagues, friends and neighbours or supporting newly baptized members of the church family.

The teaching ministry, too, cannot be the exclusive preserve of the Anglican clergy. While they do get around the parish a fair bit, vicars and priests in charge are not technically omnipresent. So who will do the teaching in the home groups dotted around the parish? Who will have the patience and the creativity to run the children's group? Who will open the Bible and unpack things theological with young people in a way that they will get? Who will do schools work when the vicar is busy taking funerals? Who will guide the man in the pub through the basics of Christianity? Who will lead the Alpha course at work? Who will take the time to sit down with the Eastern European family next door who want to know more about Jesus?

It is equally important, though, that people are not pressurized into taking on roles they feel they cannot manage. They need to be able to say no without feeling guilty. Life is super busy for 99.9% of us, work is often tiring, and our families need quality time with us. For the record, church leaders need to think carefully before asking someone to help out with this, that or the other. The point, though, is that sometimes the person with just the right gifts, in just the right place, and at just the right time might be *me*. Maybe we don't feel we've got the right gifts, that we're too inexperienced or not qualified to do x, y or z – but those who genuinely want to know more about Jesus don't tend to want an expert. What they want to know is why this Jesus makes such a difference to this or that friend, and whether Christianity 'will work' for them.[4]

Just to recap, I have suggested that in Anglicanism 'vocation' is a word that applies to all believers in so far as it concerns basic Christian discipleship. Every one of us is called to love God and neighbour, and together we are called to participate in God's mission. For many Anglicans around the world commitment to Christ can be costly. For absolutely every one of us, our 'vocation' will be about serving and sharing Jesus in public, and spending time with him in private. As we will explore below, some of us are called by God to offer the bulk of our time – and indeed our lives – to particular forms of ministry and mission. Nevertheless, the task of sharing Jesus with the world, of making disciples and of teaching the Christian faith is a responsibility we all share.

A calling within the calling

In my current role I spend a lot of time with people who are experiencing a particular calling within the general call to discipleship. The litany of likely and not so likely biblical 'heroes' is proof positive that God calls whoever he likes, whenever he likes, however he likes, and this continues to be the case today. While it's beyond the scope of this book to map out a theology of vocation, any such theology is likely to reference Paul's word to the Ephesians about God raising up 'apostles', 'prophets', 'evangelists', 'pastors' and 'teachers' in order to 'equip the saints for the work of ministry, for building up the body of Christ' (Ephesians 4.11–12).[5]

---

4 For a positive view on a pragmatic 'this works for me' approach to Christian witness, see Susan Hope, *Mission-shaped Spirituality*, London: Church House Publishing, 2006, p. 92.

5 I hope to set out some considerations on vocation to ministry and mission in the twenty-first century in a forthcoming publication.

In this quote from his letter to the Ephesians, Paul is talking about individuals who possess particular giftings from God who are commissioned within the Church to exercise a specific form of ministry for the benefit of the whole people of God. Since the earliest times, the Church in Acts that 'had all things in common' understood that every Christian must live (and die) for Jesus, but it also recognized that particular leaders should be set aside and trained to exercise spiritual leadership and public ministry.

Today the same distinction holds, and we continue to recognize that there are those who are nudged and prompted by God to step up and lead his Church. All over the Anglican world there is a difference between serving as a leader in a particular church activity, such as leading a small group or helping out at Messy Church, and becoming a recognized public minister, taking on an official role licensed by the bishop. Cathy Rowling and Paula Gooder explain the difference as follows:

> Public ministry differs from ministry in general because it carries with it the recognition and authority of the Church. Those who are involved in public ministry, to a certain extent, represent the Church and so are accountable to it. This does not imply that they are more important than others within the Church, but they do have a greater burden of responsibility. Consequently, all authorized ministry carries a licence to minister, issued under the bishop's authority, and the licence does two things: it gives permission and it makes people accountable.[6]

Precisely because licensed ministry involves 'permission', 'accountability' and ultimately the exercise of spiritual authority, when a person has an inner sense that God is calling them then this call needs to be tested. To engage in public ministry as a recognized leader, licensed by the Church – for example, as a Licensed Lay Minister (LLM), an evangelist, a pastoral assistant or as an ordained minister – certain preconditions have to be met. For

---

6 Cathy Rowling and Paula Gooder, *Reader Ministry Explored*, London: SPCK, 2009, p. 7.

instance, according to Canon E4 of the Church of England, Lay Readers, or LLMs, are entrusted with a ministry of teaching, preaching, leading services and providing pastoral support.[7] Clearly, such responsibility can't be handed out haphazardly, and those hoping to minister alongside clergy in this way will need to be supported both by their minister and PCC. Candidates for Licensed Lay Ministry usually undergo a diocesan selection process and undertake theological training.

The same is true of pastoral assistants, who engage in activities such as hospital visiting, bereavement support and marriage counselling. Accountable to the incumbent – that is, the minister in charge of a parish – and the PCC, pastoral assistants are 'Christians with a certain amount of life experience and a mature faith' who are 'trained to walk alongside others with a listening ear, especially in times of particular need'.[8] As in the case of LLMs, pastoral assistants are those who respond to a specific call to a particular form of ministry *within* the common Christian call to love and serve God and neighbour.

Again, some Provinces of the Anglican Communion are keen on training and licensing people as 'evangelists' – that is, as ministers authorized and commissioned for the specific purpose of taking a lead in evangelism. In the Anglican Church of Kenya the Church Army organization has been especially influential in training people for these roles, as it has in the Church of England.[9] Evangelists also operate as authorized ministers in Latin American countries where they are often involved in pioneering

---

7 LLM (Licensed Lay Minister) is the way the Church of England often refers to the historic office of Lay Reader.

8 As described on the website of the Diocese of Guildford: http://www.cofeguildford.org.uk/about/dvm/pastoral-assistants.

9 In the Church of England the Church Army (www.churcharmy.org) has a particular role to play and, on a national level, in October 1999 the Archbishops of Canterbury and York inaugurated the national College of Evangelists which seeks to promote evangelism throughout the Church, working across and beyond diocesan borders. The Church Army plays an important role in the Anglican Church of Kenya and in other African nations, with evangelists being trained through Carlile College (cf. www.ackenya.org).

outreach to marginalized communities and setting up networks of community support groups. Similarly, in African nations such as Mozambique and Angola, catechists are selected, given training and authorized to teach new and established members of the church community in the basics of the Christian faith.

Similarly, in most if not all Provinces of the Anglican Communion, those who wish to be ordained as either deacons or priests will embark on a journey of discernment and will submit to local/regional selection processes. In relation specifically to the discernment process around vocations to ordained ministry, there is often a national component to the selection process. Thus, when someone feels called by God to be a deacon or a priest in the Church of England, the diocesan bishop may sponsor them to attend what is known as a Bishops' Advisory Panel (BAP). At BAPs, advisers from different regions come together under the direction of personnel from the national church authority called Ministry Division. Over a couple of days these advisers assess and evaluate candidates and conclude by producing a very detailed report on the candidate, recommending to their diocesan bishop that he/she should – or should not – train for ordained ministry.

Since Scripture warns that the 'teachers' will be judged more rigorously (cf. James 3.1) it is right that the Church and the individual take the question of calling very seriously. Those who experience God's call to ordained ministry within the broader call are asked to embark on a journey of discernment and the testing of that call. The 'testing' doesn't stop there as public ministry can involve a lifetime of hard work and challenges. On the other hand, it is also an immense privilege to be able to walk alongside God's people and help the Church grow. Both the challenges and the privileges of ordained ministry are particularly apparent, we might reason, in the figure of the bishop.

What exactly do bishops do, and why do we need them?

The question sounds a little unkind, but in an apparent throwback to the vitriolic church politics of the Reformation and post-Reformation period, bishops are often viewed with suspicion by those coming from Churches that espouse a non-episcopal form of governance. Again, wider society can sometimes take this tone where there is mistrust regarding 'organized religion' or the Church as an institution. In the UK, this transpires, for example, in relation to Church of England bishops occupying seats in the House of Lords.

However, the structures of the Anglican Communion have long identified the 'historic episcopate' as one of the pillars on which Anglicanism stands (cf. Chapter 8). What's more, bishops have been a part of the life of the Church in England since the times of the Celtic saints. Indeed, in the sixth century, when the man who went on to become Augustine of Canterbury (and the first Archbishop of Canterbury) arrived in England with his entourage of 40 missionary monks, he was in for a surprise. Tasked with 'converting the Britons', though there were still plenty of pagans about, he discovered that some had already accepted the gospel and, what's more, the *ecclesia anglicana* – the English Church – had already got its own bishops.

Just as the ministry of bishops was important for the nation back then, in modern times the ministry of Anglican bishops has become a key identity marker for the Anglican Church world-wide. Indeed, one way in which the Anglican Church differs from many other expressions of Christianity is precisely in its endorsement of episcopal leadership and its commitment to, and valuing of, episcopal ministry.

In explaining what bishops do, I have found what is perhaps an unlikely analogy in martial arts. Students of karate and kung fu understand that the grand masters are rarely seen performing spectacular moves or miraculous physical manoeuvres. Again there is no pretentiousness about them, no desire to self-project or take centre stage. Fancy twisting spinning kicks, bone crushing bravado and an unflinching desire to take on the world single-handedly is the stuff of movies, not real life. In contrast, the real masters embody a quiet confidence, a normal peaceful existence and a balanced, rhythmic approach to life.

The experts stand out from other practitioners for a number of reasons. First, they are highly disciplined individuals with a proven track record – that is, they are known to dedicate themselves tirelessly to the study and practice of their art form, which they endeavour to perfect. Second, they are custodians of a tradition that has been handed down to them over centuries. As such their prime concern is to preserve that inherited wisdom by reproducing it faithfully and by teaching others to do the same. Third, they are respected members of the wider community and ambassadors for their art. As public representatives they may be called upon to explain and promote it to mainstream society and to colleagues who practise other forms. Fourth, they are tasked with the management of a geographical region; as such they are responsible for providing leadership and for mentoring and growing other leaders who operate locally. Finally, as faithful servants, they are entrusted with the task of maintaining the standards, discipline and welfare of their organization. As such, they oversee training regimes and, when necessary, step in to challenge and correct where attitudes or behaviours are going off on a tangent.

Like the grand masters of martial arts, bishops are highly motivated and disciplined leaders with a proven track record. They are individuals known to dedicate themselves tirelessly to the Lord's service, particularly prayer and the study of the Scriptures. They are guardians of the faith passed down since the apostolic era. Their prime concern is to preserve and further the gospel by adhering faithfully to it and by teaching it faithfully. This means that they are meant to be intrinsically *missional*, capable of setting out a vision and leading others in mission.

Bishops are respectable and respected members of the community, ambassadors of Jesus Christ. As public representatives, they may be called upon to explain and promote the Christian faith to religious and non-religious people alike. They are tasked with the management of a geographical region and are responsible for providing visionary leadership, mentoring and growing other leaders who operate locally. Finally, they are charged with the task of maintaining the disciplines of faithful discipleship for the good of the Church. It falls to them to step in to challenge and correct attitudes or behaviours that lead away from the truth of the gospel.

Just as the great masters of the martial arts are thoroughly grounded in the basics, eliminating any movement that is un-necessary, so our bishops are accomplished practitioners of the basics of prayer, preaching and the administering of the sacra-ments. They are competent managers because they are team players. They know how to build strong teams playing to the strengths of each team member. They are true teachers because they are truly passionate students of their subject. They exercise real care of those who are in their pastoral charge because their lives are really patterned after Jesus' life and their one goal is to live and, if necessary, die for him. They are inspirational leaders not because of any amazing feat they may have accomplished, but because of who they are in Christ.

The classic biblical description of a bishop is found in 1 Timothy 3 and has several points of contact with the portrait sketched out above:

> Now a bishop must be above reproach, married only once, temperate, sensible, respectable, hospitable, an apt teacher, not a drunkard, not violent but gentle, not quarrelsome, and not a lover of money. He must manage his own household well, keeping his children submissive and respectful in every way – for if someone does not know how to manage his own house-hold, how can he take care of God's church? He must not be a recent convert, or he may be puffed up with conceit and fall into the condemnation of the devil. Moreover, he must be well thought of by outsiders, so that he may not fall into disgrace and the snare of the devil. (1 Timothy 3.2–7)

The Greek word translated 'bishop' in the NRSV is *episcopos*, which has the basic meaning of 'overseer'. This description, then, might be taken as the minimum requirements for exercising a ministry of pastoral oversight as a bishop. It applies equally to suffragan bishops – that is, *assistant* bishops who oversee an area within a diocese; to diocesan bishops – those who oversee the life and ministry of an entire diocese; and to archbishops – those who oversee a Province, or a large geographical region consisting of several dioceses.

Within the Church of England, the website of the Diocese of Rochester contains a video where the diocesan bishop answers the question 'What does a bishop do?' Bishop James Langstaff explains that rather than 'controlling' the clergy on a day-to-day basis, his role is to 'shape things in such a way that the clergy and parishes and our chaplaincies in schools and colleges and hospitals and prisons can do their work well'.[10] As expressed in the video, this *shaping* so as to ensure the spiritual health and efficacy of those in the bishop's care is founded on prayer. If the bishop is to shape the mission and life of God's people, then he or she must be shaped by God and that means being rooted in prayer. Again, responsible oversight involves leading by example, and following in the footsteps of Christ it means servant leadership.

Missing our vocation?

Earlier we explored the idea that the Great Commission applies to every Christian, not just, for example, mission partners in Morocco, a priest preparing candidates for confirmation, or a bishop working out a strategy for growth. Both in the UK and in South America I have heard faithful Christians lament that they are unable to help out with this or that church event because of family commitments, that they 'can't do more' because of work. Such people feel embarrassed by their apparent lack of involvement in the local church, but nine times out of ten they (and

10 See www.rochester.anglican.org/communications/news/what-does-a-bishop-do.php.

overbearing clergy) have overlooked a remarkably obvious truth. Namely, that by living openly for Jesus in their place of work and/ or in the family, they are being faithful to Christ as committed members of the Church – that is, Church with a capital 'C', meaning God's people everywhere and throughout history.

That so many people can miss the significance of their Christian presence at work or in their street suggests that our entire church culture needs changing. The Church of England General Synod Paper GS2056, 'Setting God's People Free', draws attention to how churches in the UK have often become too inward-focused and narrow in their understanding of vocation and mission. It cites the contrast of the Sunday school teacher who is regularly prayed over at the front of the church, and the school teacher sitting in the pew who is passionate about modelling Christ to her pupils five days a week – but is never prayed for on a Sunday.[11]

For many Christian teachers, quite rightly, teaching is their *vocation*. It is their vocation in the secular sense – where the term still carries very positive connotations – but more than that it is their vocation in a Christian sense as it involves modelling the values of Jesus, showing God's love to children, and preparing future generations to engage with society and promote the common good. It's not hard to see that with different nuancing, the very same might be said of the health professions or those who work in politics or the criminal justice system and of other public service workers. But why stop there at the obvious ones?

Mark, one of my closest friends, worked for a time in a builders' yard. Now, Mark wouldn't say that the particular job he was doing was his *vocation in life,* but for a time it was a vocation of sorts. Since he was the only Christian working in the firm, it didn't take long for people to realize there was something different about him. Excepting, perhaps, the occasional slip-up,

---

11 The General Synod Report 'Setting God's People Free' (GS2056) sets the agenda for a change in culture regarding vocations in the Church of England. The report is downloadable at the following: https://www.churchofengland. org/renewal-reform/setting-gods-people-free.aspx.

he didn't swear, didn't get drunk, and he didn't boast about his popularity with the opposite sex. In the years that Mark worked in the builders' yard he had many very real conversations about Jesus with some very tough men. On occasion, trying not to be spotted by the others, some would ask for prayer. Gradually, seeing how Jesus was so real in Mark's life, one or two of them swallowed their pride and agreed to do a discipleship course – as long as Mark went along too, which he did. It isn't that the entire builders' yard came to faith in Jesus, but one or two did. Ironically, Mark was someone who was regularly pressured by finger-pointing church leaders because he wasn't 'doing enough'.

Another example in an overseas Anglican context was a man, who, for a time, was one of my parishioners. Coming to faith through the Cursillo Movement (a movement started in the Roman Catholic Church, but now common in Anglicanism), Jesus revolutionized the life of this successful businessman. His *vocation in life* was business. As a teenager he had begun at the bottom selling fruit ice-lollies, but after a few years he had put together a small firm that had mushroomed into one of the region's most successful ice-cream producers. Realizing that his Christian vocation need not be separate from his work life, he began to hold services at lunchtimes and prayer breakfasts for his workers. Many came to faith and, in the meantime, a new business venture of fruit drinks was an instant success and made millions. An interesting detail is that this disciple of Jesus was able to practise his discipleship by offering some of his business acumen and horticultural know-how to a poor parish in a rural setting. With his help, they learned to grow crops successfully and managed to set up a cooperative, bringing a new quality of life to a rural community.

There are many more such examples that might be quoted, but the point I hope is clear. For all our talk of reaching others in the community and 'making a difference', we clergy have sometimes overlooked the fact that in different ways the people sitting right in front of us are doing this day in day out. Those tasked with leading our churches need to be asking their congregations how they as leaders might support them in the *things they are already doing*, rather than hounding them into volunteering for various activities they don't want to be involved in. Instead the questions should be, 'How can the church support the supermarket worker who longs to share Jesus with her workmates?' Or, 'How can the church make the most of links that are on its very doorstep?'

Good church leadership will look for the natural openings for the gospel that arise from, and in, the congregation. Wise leadership will seek to pray into and move into those opportunities by the grace of God. Similarly, healthy leadership teams will encourage and release others into positions of influence and strategic importance. Ultimately, while God calls who he wants, whenever he wants, and however he wants, he wants us to work together and no one is asked to go it alone.

For what it's worth, the priest who thinks she's supposed to lead singlehandedly every local initiative, coordinate every Alpha course, serve at every soup run, sit on every committee, oversee every prayer meeting, run every small group, preach at all four services, and convert every soul in the town is doing no one any favours. Apart from the fact that hyperactive priests are on a one-way ticket to burnout, the 'leave it to me, it's no bother' instinct denies gifted people the opportunity to deploy their gifts in God's service. It denies people the chance to grow and it stifles the expansion of the kingdom.

So, just run over again, what do Anglicans understand by 'vocation' and 'calling'?

In this chapter we have seen how all Christians are called to follow Jesus, to share his love and his life in their day-to-day lives. Just as Jesus makes the difference to us, we are to make a difference for him in our attitudes, actions and words. This calling is a calling to a life of discipleship, of letting go of our self-centred way of life, in order to align ourselves with Christ and the ethic and agenda of the kingdom of God. It's about allowing ourselves to be transformed by the power of God's Spirit that we in turn may be transformative. Our common vocation isn't played out in the silence of the monastery: the rubber hits the road in the hustle and bustle of a noisy and needy world.

There are, of course, those who experience a call within that broader call to follow Christ. Anglicanism has a spectrum of public ministries, both lay and ordained, that individuals are called into. Licensed ministers are no better and no holier than other Christians – though they should have particular spiritual giftings that enable them to help lead the Church. They also bear a greater weight of responsibility as those appointed to exercise spiritual authority. This is particularly true of bishops who, as we have seen, have a special contribution to make.

Finally, we observed that many Anglicans have a vocation in terms of their profession and work life. Church leaders must encourage and equip each person to be an effective voice for Jesus in the place where they live and work.

Questions for individual or group reflection

1 In what sense do Christians have a common vocation and what is that vocation about?
2 What do you think a life of discipleship and of following Jesus requires?
3 Which are the giftings that you feel God has given to you (perhaps these are 'natural' abilities and/or spiritual gifts)?
4 Who do you know who has experienced 'a call within the call', and could you chat to them about how they came to sense it and act on it?
5 Why has the Anglican Church always valued the office and ministry of bishops?

7

How do Anglicans *do* mission?

Mission is so important to Anglicans around the world that our global family has taken the trouble to sit round the table and deliberate over exactly what we mean by the word 'mission'. Developed by the Anglican Consultative Council, one of the bodies of the Anglican Communion, work on the 'Five Marks of Mission' began in 1984. The Five Marks of Mission were received at the Lambeth Conference of 1988 and were used as a resource for a key theme – 'the Bishop in Mission' – 20 years later at the 2008 Lambeth Conference.[1] They were formally adopted by the Church of England's General Synod in 1996, and many overseas provinces and dioceses have similarly made them integral to their missional life.

Thus, on the Anglican Communion website you will find resources on the Five Marks of Mission produced by the likes of the Diocese of Montreal, the Diocese of Bermuda and the Anglican Church in Myanmar.[2]

The Five Marks of Mission are:

1 To proclaim the good news of the kingdom.
2 To teach, baptize and nurture new believers.
3 To respond to human need by loving service.

---

1 Information drawn from David Walker, *God's Belongers*, Abingdon: Bible Reading Fellowship, 2017, p. 92.

2 See www.anglicancommunion.org/identity/marks-of-mission/resources. aspx.

4 To transform unjust structures of society, to challenge violence of every kind and pursue peace and reconciliation.
5 To strive to safeguard the integrity of creation, and sustain and renew the life of the earth.[3]

Perhaps the first thing that strikes us about this five-pronged definition/description of mission is just how wide-ranging and comprehensive it is. Anyone who has studied missiology will detect in it the influence of the Pact of Lausanne (1974), which, under the influence of the famous Anglican thinker and writer John Stott, called on Christians to take a broader view of mission than they had previously done. Because God is the author and sustainer of life, every level of human and earthly life *matters*. The message of the gospel speaks as much to society as it does to the individual; it is directed as much to *this life* as it is to the afterlife. It is about the individual, but it is also about creation and the universe in its breathtaking enormity. It is about the here and now, but in addition it is about how we got to today and what tomorrow will look like.

More than just a description, the Five Marks are effectively a 'manifesto for mission', setting out a pattern for life and action for all Anglicans. They begin in marks 1 and 2 with the directives of Jesus' Great Commission in Matthew 28.19–20. Thus, the first two marks have to do mainly with *evangelism* – that is, the verbal proclamation of the good news of the saving and life-giving death and resurrection of Jesus Christ. On an Anglican understanding, then, evangelism is a key element of mission. Some might feel it to be the number one priority of mission, but most would agree that the Five Marks are not intended to be a ranking system. Instead, the five are to be taken together as one, and in this way *every aspect* of our mission carries within it evangelistic potentiality.

Mark 3 – responding to human need by loving service – may be said to flow naturally from mark 1. What better way to communicate the good news of the kingdom of God than by meeting

---

3 See the 'identity' section of the official website of the Anglican Communion: www.anglicancommunion.org.

people where they are and responding in love to their needs? It's not that 'actions speak louder than words', but words speak louder when backed up by action. Time and time again we see Jesus in the Gospels responding to human need in loving service. They're hungry, he feeds them. They're ill, he heals them. They're vulnerable, he protects them. They're lonely, he befriends them. Unlike the Pharisees, Jesus' words are backed up by his actions.

This leads us neatly on to mark 4, 'To transform unjust structures of society, to challenge violence of every kind and pursue peace and reconciliation'. An absolutely crucial headline of the good news of the kingdom of God is that transformation of individuals, societies and nations is not just a possibility, but the firm purpose and plan of God. With the cross and resurrection at the centre of human history, where God's Spirit is at work transformation occurs and people, society and nations are magnetically drawn towards the centre. Left to its own devices, society is a mess because human existence is messy. Nevertheless, just as Jesus worked to transform the unjust structure of his society, Christians are called and equipped by the Spirit to transform the rotten structures of the societies in which they live. 'Blessed are the peacemakers,' Jesus taught his disciples, so it falls to us to confront violence wherever we find it and doggedly pursue peace and reconciliation, even when humanly speaking the going seems slow.

Finally, mark 5 urges us to 'safeguard the integrity of creation' and to 'sustain and renew the life of the earth'. In recent years, leading Anglican theologians such as N. T. (Tom) Wright have written and spoken extensively about how for centuries Christians have misread the New Testament, imagining that in the world to come we'll be floating around on fluffy clouds plucking away at our harps in a cartoon-like heaven.[4] Crucially, where the Bible speaks about our future life, it speaks not only about 'new heavens' but also of a 'new earth' where the emphasis is on a *renewed* earth (cf.

---

4 See, for example, Tom Wright, *Simply Christian*, London: SPCK, 2006; cf. N. T. Wright, *The New Testament and the People of God*, London: SPCK, 1992, pp. 298–300.

Romans 8.19–21; Revelation 21).[5] There is a physicality about the age to come that is recognizably the revamping and total healing of our earth – therefore what we do *now* matters for later.

God created the world and, as Genesis stresses to the nth degree, he created it 'good'. Just as Adam and Eve are tasked with tending the garden, humankind is tasked with stewarding the planet – that is, 'safeguarding the integrity of creation'. God has chosen us to partner with him in overseeing the earth and working for its future renewal. Since we've made such a mess of that over the last few centuries, it is apt that our principal Anglican mission statement puts this squarely back on the agenda.

The Five Marks of Mission in action

In the early 2000s I served as a lay reader, and then as curate, in the Parish of the Living Waters in Olinda, Brazil.[6] The church grew out of a mission plant aimed at reaching some of the poorest and most marginalized members of a large Brazilian city. When the plant got going in the 1990s, the community it strove to reach was eking out a miserable existence working on the city rubbish dump. Sometimes people even *lived* on the dump in makeshift shelters. Children who should have been in school were trawling through waste, exposed to disease, and danger in the form of bulldozers. Elderly men and women who should have been relaxing into retirement instead picked their way through the refuse in the wilting tropical heat, gathering recyclable materials that could be sold on for a meagre sum. Some families were so poor they were forced to feed on the scraps of food they found on the immense mountain of putrefying waste.

---

5 This nuance was stressed by Bishop Graham Cray in his addresses to the Diocese of Winchester in its Diocesan Conference in 2016.

6 For an account of some of the activities this parish got off the ground, see Marcus Throup, 'Learning to Be: A Brazilian Case Study in Social Injustice', *Common Ground Journal*, 3.2, 2006, available at: http://www.commonground journal.org/volnum/vo3no2.pdf.

From the outset the strategy of the church was to proclaim the good news with both words and actions, responding to acute human need with loving service. The very first service embodied this approach, holding together marks 1–3 of the Five Marks. It took place on the dump itself and as the preaching finished Christian medical professionals stepped forward to offer free health checks and medicines to the impoverished, who were stunned that people were taking an interest in them.

Over time, at the request of the community of *catadores* – those who hunt for recyclable materials – a church building was set up close to the dump. Through the work of the Anglican Church, who put pressure on the local authorities who had turned a blind eye to the hundreds living on and around the refuse, many in the community were housed. Again, church leaders became increasingly aware of corruption and problems with government structures (cf. mark 4) and, notwithstanding threats – including death threats – the church stood up for the rights of the oppressed.

After several years, partnering with NGOs and other organizations in order to work for the common good, this church helped end child labour on the dump. It also began to provide social programmes for the families and young people of the area. These included health services, education and support groups. For example, a Christian dentist gave free treatment in a building belonging to the church, and education practitioners offered courses to the young people in music, basic literacy, numeracy and computing. Whereas young people outside the church often got involved in drug gangs and the violence associated with them, those who came into the church were given the tools to move forward in life and they began to become agents of change in their society. Many of the young people who were part of the group that my wife and I led are now in full-time employment and have thriving families of their own. This would have been simply unimaginable before the church arrived on the scene.

In the meantime, leaders from the parish began to push for change for those working on the dump. Conscious of the Fifth

Mark of Mission, the church started to explore ways in which the wider society might value the work of those who toiled on the dump in conjunction with the recycling industry – after all, they were working hard in the business of sustaining and renewing the planet. The church also pushed for better working conditions, and was instrumental in setting up and supporting a recycling cooperative. After several years the open dump became a real landfill site with proper regulation of working conditions and workers' rights.

Naturally, it is one thing to describe these transformative results but quite another to go into the detail of the arduous journey to change. Challenges, obstacles and opposition were part and parcel of the day-to-day mission carried out in the area. When I was part of the leadership team, along with my incumbent Simea, frequently I felt angered by the neglect of local author-ities and powerless to make a difference. But in his goodness and graciousness, over time God brought change to that com-munity as individually and together they met Jesus. In just over a decade, the parish had an active adult membership of a couple of hundred people, many of whom were under the age of 30, and innumerable children who were very much a part of the vibrancy of church life. Moreover, the church was at the centre of the com-munity and the beating heart of everything that was making a difference to the people of that place.

Notwithstanding the very real challenges, the missional work of the Anglican Church in Olinda illustrates how the Five Marks of Mission translate into concrete change.[7] A proper Anglican approach must hold together both the word and the deed of the gospel. Our bishop had a memorable catchphrase that became a missional principle: 'no parish without a social project, and no social project without a parish'. That, for me, is at the heart of what the Five Marks of Mission are getting at.

---

7 For a discussion of the Five Marks of Mission in relation to the UK con-text, see David Walker, *God's Belongers*, Abingdon: Bible Reading Fellowship, 2017, pp. 92–104.

Anglican movements and mission

While the Five Marks of Mission are still quite new, the missio-
logical principles that undergird them have emerged in various
historical Anglican movements which, in their own ways, became
a force for world mission. There isn't scope to look at all the
different movements that have played a part here, so rather than
picking a relatively well-known movement such as Methodism, I
have picked one that is often overlooked in relation to *mission* –
namely, the Oxford Movement.

The Oxford Movement began in the 1830s when the British government admitted nonconformist (i.e. non-Anglican) Members
of Parliament and seemed to be making rulings that limited the
authority and influence of the Church of England. In protest,
Oxford academics such as John Henry Newman and John Keble
published tracts (thus he and his colleagues came to be known
as 'tractarians') in a bid to restore the authority of the Church of
England on the grounds of apostolic succession – the belief that
the ordination of Anglican clergy can be traced in an unbroken
line all the way back to the apostles. Since the authority of the
Church came from God himself, they argued, only those commissioned in the line of the apostles could claim to be his legitimate
representatives on earth. In effect, the so-called tractarians were
resisting nonconformist influences in the Houses of Parliament
and arguing that only the Church of England possessed divine
authority. They were also concerned to recover an emphasis on
the holy and sacramental aspects of Anglicanism, not least in the
light of evangelical and 'low church' influences in Britain and
beyond.

Since it was so tied to events in England it is perhaps surprising that
the influence of the Oxford Movement and its Anglo-Catholicism
was felt beyond the shores of the Church of England. Nevertheless, in some ways it became a force for world mission. In
Africa, for instance, Anglo-Catholic missionaries helped establish national Churches like the Church of the Province of South
Africa. In some countries the Anglo-Catholic emphasis on the

holiness and authority of God's Church fuelled challenges against unjust political and social conditions – exactly the kind of thing envisaged today in mark 4 of the Five Marks. For example, the struggle for racial equality and an end to apartheid in South Africa was one in which Anglo-Catholic leaders were heavily involved. For those of us old enough to remember news footage of protests against apartheid, those scenes of the iconic figure of Archbishop Desmond Tutu soon come to mind.[8]

Clearly, the Oxford Movement and its overseas incarnations had a political dimension, but it was a religious movement at heart. A central concern of early Anglo-Catholicism was to elevate the standing of the priest and to recover a sense of holiness and piety through the restoration of traditional ritual and sacramental practices.[9] Given that this was in part a reaction against 'low church' evangelicalism, it is significant that in more recent times a leading Anglican evangelical scholar can describe the Oxford Movement as a 'renewing influence bringing new life to the church and its worship'.[10] However, I would go a step further and acknowledge that the Oxford Movement was a force for world mission.

In addition to its missional impact in South Africa, in the mid-1800s the Oxford Movement also had a strong influence in the USA. Professor Samuel Wells observes that the 'Reformed Episcopal Church' was established by evangelically minded North Americans in response to what they perceived to be objectionable Catholic tendencies arising from the Oxford Movement.[11] The flip side of that coin is that many clergy who remained in the Episcopal Church espoused a positive view of the

---

8 This paragraph is dependent on Michael Nazir-Ali's chapter 'A Worldwide Communion', in Ian Bunting (ed.), *Celebrating the Anglican Way*, London: Grove Books, 1996, p. 58.

9 There was a shift back towards more Roman Catholic ways – for instance, Anglo-Catholicism had recourse to the 1549 prayer book.

10 Alister E. McGrath, *The Renewal of Anglicanism*, London: SPCK, 1993, p. 30.

11 Samuel Wells, *What Anglicans Believe*, Norwich: Canterbury Press, 2011, p. 102.

liturgical developments taking place in England, and embraced an Anglo-Catholic spirituality as part of their mission and ministry.

This had a knock-on effect in overseas mission carried out by American Episcopalians. Thus, in the late nineteenth century Episcopalian missionaries from the famed West Virginia Seminary established an Anglo-Catholic legacy in Brazil. To this day, the spirituality of the Brazilian Episcopal Church (IEAB) stands in marked contrast to the Anglican Churches in other South American countries, which were mainly founded by evangelical missionaries from England and have a very different spirituality. That does not mean, however, that the Anglo-Catholic missionaries were any less fervent. Towards the end of the nineteenth century, at considerable personal risk – that is, from hostile Roman Catholic groups – after just a few years' service missionary bishops Kinsolving and Morris confirmed upwards of 12,000 new Anglicans. While the Anglican Church in Brazil is still a long way off from reaching its true potential, the legacy of Kinsolving and Morris lives on today.[12]

So, how does Anglicanism approach mission?

So far we have looked at the Five Marks of Mission and seen them acted out in a contemporary global Anglican context. We have also sketched the missional impact of the Oxford Movement and seen that the principles drawn up in the Five Marks had something of a pre-history in these (and other) movements. There is, though, a more fundamental question hinted at in the title of the chapter – is mission simply something we *do* or should it be about the very people we are?

In recent years it has been commonplace to talk about *missio Dei* – a Latin phrase that translates as 'the mission of God'. What

---

12 For a fuller perspective on Brazilian Anglicanism, see G. L. C. Branco and Marcus Throup, 'The Anglican Episcopal Church of Brazil', in *The Wiley-Blackwell Companion to the Anglican Communion*, Oxford: Blackwell, 2013, pp. 539–46.

it indicates is that all true Christian mission *belongs* to God and is rooted in the very being of God himself. Not only does it *belong* to God, but in so far as all that is truly good comes from God, mission is his initiative, his miracle and his prerogative. So, mission isn't just something Christians *do*, it's much more fundamental than that. Mission is at the heart of who God *is* and it follows, therefore, that it must also be at the heart of what it means to be a Christian.

Questions for individual or group reflection

1 What was your understanding of the term 'mission' before you read this chapter, and how has that understanding altered (if at all)?
2 What is your own experience of 'mission' and to what extent is your local church engaged in mission?
3 Which do you think is the most important mark of mission? Should the Five Marks of Mission be seen as a hierarchy or are they equally important?
4 'If everything is "mission" nothing is'; how would you respond to this comment?
5 What do you make of the idea that God himself is *missional*?

8

How does the worldwide Anglican Communion work?

On 24 September 1867, a conference of bishops met in Lambeth in London to address some challenges affecting the Anglican Church overseas. In so doing, for the first time people began to think of Anglicanism as a global expression of Christianity. Curiously, the controversial issues that gave rise to the first Lambeth Conference provide a parallel to issues that have resurfaced in recent years – namely, disagreements over human sexuality and questions regarding the jurisdiction of bishops and the autonomy of dioceses.

The issue underlying the first Lambeth Conference was the controversy surrounding John Colenso, the Bishop of Natal in South Africa. Colenso had argued for the tolerance of polygamy among African converts and also denied orthodox teaching on salvation and the message of the cross. Opposed by bishops both in South Africa and England, Colenso had been deposed by the Bishop of Cape Town. However, after an appeal to the Privy Council in London, it was ruled in Colenso's favour that Cape Town had no authority to wade in with regard to the affairs of Natal. Eventually, an anomalous situation came about whereby Colenso continued as bishop, but was no longer recognized by the other South African bishops who set up a parallel diocese in Natal with a new bishop.

Again, this odd set of circumstances curiously foreshadows developments 150 years later where Anglicans in Brazil and North America have become divided over the question of sexuality and the Church. In the same geographical region, some recognize the authority of one bishop while others contest it, pledging allegiance to another bishop who provides 'alternative oversight'. Tragically, bitter lawsuits have been fought out between rival Anglican groups and the pastoral fall-out has been substantial.

Although the Lambeth Conference of 1867 discussed several topics, because of the 'Colenso affair' it had no option but to wrestle with the structural and institutional difficulties relating to the jurisdiction, autonomy and accountability of diocesan bishops. It had become clear that the worldwide family of Anglican Churches would continue to meet these sorts of cultural challenges as a result of its broad diversity, but also because of its organizational make-up.

At the first Lambeth Conference, the bishops were keen to preserve unity and establish common beliefs and values that they could all sign up to. In some matters, such as polygamy, a Province might be persuaded to relinquish a national custom in the interests of international unity. After the 1867 Conference, subsequent ones developed the notion of a united family of worldwide Anglican Churches. Let's take a look at how the Anglican Communion emerged and developed.

The Anglican Communion: origins and direction of travel

To put it crudely but reasonably accurately, Anglican Churches came into being wherever the English settled overseas for reasons of trade and commerce, or where the British Empire developed its colonies. Overseas chaplaincies were established to serve expats in colonial lands and also in foreign territories where British communities had settled for reasons of trade and commerce – for example, Brazil and Argentina in the nineteenth century. These chaplaincies tended to be inward-looking and concerned with the spiritual well-being of the expat community. The conversion of the locals was not part of the remit, and in predominantly Roman Catholic countries 'proselytism' was strictly prohibited.

In contrast, outside of overseas chaplaincy work, the empire afforded opportunities to enterprising groups and individuals who felt called to global mission. In the heyday of colonial Britain, thousands of missionaries set sail for distant lands to proclaim the gospel of Christ and convert indigenous peoples.

Founded in 1701, the Anglican Society for the Propagation of the Gospel sent missionaries to support Anglicans in America and the West Indies and to share the gospel with Indians and descendants of African slaves. A century later the Anglican Evangelical Church Missionary Society was formed, later becoming known as the Church Missionary Society (CMS). Its missionary endeavours in India and Africa played a major part in establishing national Churches and encouraging indigenous leaders, and it continues to work in this way right up to the present day.

It is from this context of colonial churches and overseas mission efforts that the Anglican Communion began to emerge in the latter part of the nineteenth century. From the 1867 Lambeth Conference onwards, Anglicanism began to emerge as a global expression of Christianity; but although the British Empire had been a vehicle for Anglican missionary initiatives around the globe, American and Canadian bishops were adamant that the Anglican Communion would be no *church empire*. They insisted that the Communion was to be a family for all – there were to be no Union Jacks under the cassocks, and no neo-colonial agendas hiding behind the dog collars!

Initially focused around the English-speaking Churches, over time the Communion sought to include Anglican Churches from around the globe. Nevertheless, in many nations bishops were expat missionaries rather than home-grown leaders. Famously, though, through the efforts of CMS pioneers, Samuel Ajayi Crowther (*c.* 1809–91) was consecrated bishop, and then became Archbishop of Nigeria. Crowther's remarkable journey from a Portuguese *negreiro* (slave ship) to Sierra Leone, London and eventually back to Nigeria as the first Anglican African bishop is movingly inspirational. Sadly, though, it took a very long time before the consecration of national leaders as bishops became the norm. The first Anglican Bishop of Brazil was a North American consecrated in 1890, but the first Brazilian bishop was consecrated almost 50 years later, in 1935, and he was a suffragan (assistant) bishop. Other Anglican Churches in South America have only recently begun appointing indigenous leaders as bishops.

Just as members of the same family usually bear a resemblance to one another, have certain things in common and are broadly accountable to one another, the Churches of the Anglican Communion would be united around a set of common characteristics and values. At first implicitly, and later more explicitly, there was an impetus to foster mutual accountability in terms of moving forward together as companions in God's mission. Over time, bishops would regard one another as equals and colleagues in Christ. During the years I served as International Secretary of an overseas diocese, I related closely to bishops from North America, South America, Africa and occasionally Asia, and when they gathered there was definitely a sense of collegiality and mutual respect.

In historical terms, the shared traits and 'house rules' of the Anglican family were set out many years ago in something that came to be known as the Chicago-Lambeth Quadrilateral. To unpack this bizarre-sounding jargon, the 'Chicago-Lambeth' part simply indicates where the statement of shared principles was first worked out (Chicago), and then adopted (Lambeth – at the 1888 conference). The 'Quadrilateral' is the four-pillar foundation on which Anglican identity and unity stands. The four pillars are:

1 The Holy Scriptures of the Old and New Testaments, as 'containeth all things necessary to salvation', and as being the rule and ultimate standard of faith.
2 The Apostles' Creed, as the baptismal symbol; and the Nicene Creed, as the sufficient statement of the Christian faith.
3 The two sacraments ordained by Christ himself – baptism and the Supper of the Lord – ministered with unfailing use of Christ's words of institution, and of the elements ordained by him.

4 The historic episcopate, locally adapted in the methods of its administration to the varying needs of the nations and peoples called of God into the unity of his Church.

As the first attempt to pin down a common trans-global Anglican identity this was fresh, but it's equally true that there was no reinventing of the wheel here. In point of fact, the first three pillars of the Quadrilateral build very clearly on principles set out within the '39 Articles of Religion' (included at the back of this book).[1] The 'Articles' are a belief statement based on Archbishop Thomas Cranmer's attempts to clarify points of doctrine at the time of the English Reformation. They were amended in the latter part of the sixteenth century under Archbishop Matthew Parker and included in the Book of Common Prayer of 1662.

As in the 39 Articles (Article 6 of which is quoted in the first pillar of the Quadrilateral), the very first thing to be ascertained is the central importance of the Bible for Christian belief and life (the first pillar above). Both historically and theologically, this is a very *Anglican* thing. Even before the Reformation, English theologians such as John Wycliffe were keen to translate the Scriptures and have them read to the people in a language they could comprehend – that is, English – as opposed to gabbling at them in what to them would be mysterious gobbledegook – that is, Latin. At the Reformation this concern came to the fore, albeit partly for political reasons.

Again, following the sequence found in the 39 Articles, the second pillar of the Quadrilateral holds up the Apostles' Creed and the Nicene Creed as 'the sufficient statement of the Christian faith'. In other words, the truths set out in the creeds provide an effective summary of what Anglicans believe. The third pillar of the Quadrilateral places emphasis on the significance of the

---

1 It is therefore misleading when Chapman states in relation to the Quadrilateral, 'there was no mention of ... the Thirty-Nine Articles'; see M. Chapman, *Anglicanism: A Very Short Introduction*, Oxford: Oxford University Press, 2006, p. 121.

sacraments of Holy Baptism and 'the Supper of the Lord' – that is, Holy Communion (cf. Article 28 of the 39 Articles).

The fourth pillar introduces something slightly different: the 'historic episcopate'; that is, the governance of the Church through bishops becomes a key identity marker and defining characteristic of the Anglican Church (cf. Chapter 5). The stress on contextualization – that is, that the episcopate must be *locally adapted ... to the varying needs of the nations* – reflects a changing culture and a radical paradigm shift. Many Anglican Churches worldwide may have begun life within a predominantly British top-down colonial model of control, but over time efforts were being made to replace this with a more grassroots post-colonial model of collaboration.

If we fast forward 100 years from the final decades of the nineteenth century to the early years of the twenty-first century, what does the Anglican Communion look like? At the Lambeth Conference in 2008, the bishops of the Anglican Communion gathered for prayer and for joint reflection on the issues facing the Church and the world. In 2008, 660 bishops were present, representing every part of the Anglican world. A glance at photos taken at the event reveals an important development: increasingly the Churches of the Anglican Communion have appointed indigenous bishops. Thus, the fourth pillar of the Quadrilateral has become a concrete reality, not just an ideal.

Again, in an unprecedented way the Lambeth Conference of 2008 celebrated the multination multi-ethnic composition of the Communion in its inaugural Holy Communion service:

> The choir sang a setting, not from the usual repertoire of English cathedral music, but from Congolese music. The epistle was read in Korean, while the gospel was read in French by a deacon from the Cameroon ... The intercessions, based on the Scottish form, were offered in Hindi, Portuguese, Japanese and French.[2]

---

2 Kenneth Stevenson, 'Anglican Aesthetics' (pp. 165–75), in Mark D. Chapman, Sathianathan Clarke and Martyn Percy (eds), *The Oxford Handbook of Anglican Studies*, Oxford: Oxford University Press, 2016, p. 166.

Bringing together such a wonderful array of cultural and ethnic diversity across the 165 nations in which the Anglican Church exists, the decennial Lambeth Conference is one of four 'instruments' that promote unity in the Anglican Communion. The 'instruments of unity' are:

1 The Archbishop of Canterbury
2 The Lambeth Conference
3 The Anglican Consultative Council (ACC)
4 The Primates' Meeting

The Archbishop of Canterbury is a figurehead and focus for unity within the Anglican Communion. The Lambeth Conference is a forum for, and the fulcrum of, Anglican unity; its 'Resolutions' cover all kinds of areas from human sexuality to global warming, providing broad guidelines for Anglican attitudes and approaches to contemporary issues. The Anglican Consultative Council (ACC) is a body presided over by the Archbishop of Canterbury made up of representatives from each Anglican Province, including bishops, clergy and laity. The ACC meets every three to four years and is tasked with aiding the Communion to achieve its main objectives as expressed in the Lambeth Conference and in the Primates' Meeting. The Primates' Meeting, like the ACC, is presided over by the Archbishop of Canterbury. It gathers archbishops to address particular issues in an advisory capacity, and meetings are attended by one representative from each national Church.

Without getting lost in the detail, this thumbnail sketch of the 'instruments of unity' invites a couple of quick observations. First, it's clear that, with the Archbishop of Canterbury occupying a central position, there is a lot of overlap and convergence between the four instruments of unity. The instruments, it seems, pay careful attention to the ancient proverb, 'Without counsel, plans go wrong, but with many advisers they succeed' (Proverbs 15.22). On the other hand, with so much overlap, it is sometimes difficult to determine who makes the final decisions and who holds who to account. One instrument may approach a matter in a different way to another and, more pointedly, it is difficult to know which (if any) instrument has the power to *enforce* decisions or apply discipline. We will touch on some of these issues below.

'Elephants in the room' – a Communion in crisis?

Back in 2003, the decision taken by the Episcopal Church in the USA to consecrate as bishop a man in an active homosexual relationship was celebrated by some and lamented by others. For one group, based largely in the developed West, it represented a step forward, the overdue beginning of a new era of change and inclusion in the Church. For the American Episcopalians who made this bold move, everything was done in accordance with their canons and consciences and, crucially, it was done in conversation with their culture. For many others, however, this was a step backwards from the conversations on human sexuality at the 1998 Lambeth Conference, enshrined in Lambeth Resolution 1.10, and a departure from orthodox Christian belief. Whatever else it did, this historic consecration in the USA deepened the disagreement over human sexuality and resulted in a distressing disunity in the Communion.

At a global level, the majority of Anglicans who maintain a traditional view on human sexuality looked to Canterbury for a lead but, under the circumstances, what could the then archbishop Rowan Williams do? Everyone is clear that the Archbishop of Canterbury is not an Anglican version of the Pope. Anglicans do not regard their affectionately abbreviated 'ABC' as infallible, nor does he issue dogmas or decrees that are to be observed in all the Anglican Churches worldwide. Nevertheless, within the Anglican Communion the Archbishop of Canterbury does have a special symbolic leadership role among the bishops in which he is recognized as *primus inter pares* – 'first among equals'.

Since, then, the Archbishop of Canterbury is a symbol of unity for the Anglican Communion and one of the four so-called 'instruments of unity' of the Communion – arguably the pivotal instrument – conservative Anglicans felt that he could and should wade into the deepening crisis. In the early 2000s, conservatives petitioned Rowan Williams to take a proactive hands-on approach to intervene in disputes in Brazil and in the USA. Seemingly, though, that was not an approach that the Archbishop felt he could take.

The problem with an interventionist-type approach was that it would seem to undermine what is sometimes known as the 'Principal of Subsidiarity' – namely, the very Anglican idea that important decisions are made at a local level rather than imposed from outside or from above. The Anglican/Episcopal Churches who were in the process of rewriting their canons – that is, church laws – to reflect a new more inclusive understanding of marriage/family were aware of this, and stressed the autonomy of each Province. The message from them was that Canterbury ought to keep its distance, and this ultimately is what happened.

Growing dissatisfaction with the lack of clear disciplinary action against the Episcopal Church in the USA prompted the birth of the conservative movement GAFCON – Global Anglican Future Conference. With a strong contingent of bishops, particularly African bishops, it gathered in Jerusalem in 2008 and distanced itself from Canterbury in the so-called Jerusalem Declaration.[3] By this time America itself had become split. The Episcopal Church of the United States of America (ECUSA) became TEC (The Episcopal Church). Since 2003, the majority of those who maintain a traditional stance on issues in human sexuality had felt unable to be a part of TEC, and felt they were being driven out. Many former Episcopalians have made their home in ACNA (Anglican Communion in North America). ACNA is something of a parallel provincial structure which, while not technically

---

3 In regard to the divisions in the Anglican Church in Brazil, see G. L.C. Branco and Marcus Throup, 'The Anglican Episcopal Church of Brazil', in *The Wiley-Blackwell Companion to the Anglican Communion*, Oxford: Blackwell, 2013, pp. 539–46. For a brief statement of the background to the rift over sexuality in the Episcopal Church in the USA, see Samuel Wells, *What Anglicans Believe*, Norwich: Canterbury Press, 2011, pp. 106–7.

a member of the Anglican Communion, has sometimes been included in official meetings.[4]

Arguably, the present Archbishop of Canterbury, Justin Welby, has been more interventionist than his predecessor – for example, imposing certain restrictions on TEC and opting not to convene the 2018 Lambeth Conference.[5] Nevertheless, the locus of the Archbishop's attempt to address the Anglican homosexuality crisis has been the Primates' Meeting. As noted, established in 1978, the Primates' Meeting gathers the *primates* – that is, the archbishops of the Provinces of the Communion – to reflect prayerfully on issues facing the Communion. At recent meetings senior Anglican bishops have committed to 'walking together' – that is, while recognizing there are disagreements over issues in human sexuality, and principally homosexuality, they have pledged to strive together to preserve the unity of the Anglican Communion.

So, how does the worldwide Anglican Communion work?

The worldwide Anglican Communion works as a global partner-ship and is committed to the mutual flourishing of its member Churches. The Communion and/or Anglicanism allows for much diversity in all sorts of ways, but at the same time it strives to preserve *unity* in diversity and celebrates that which we have in common. The Lambeth Quadrilateral consists of four 'markers' that mark out our common Anglican identity in fairly broad terms. The ethos of a vibrant diversity undergirded by a core unity is borne out in the Anglican Communion in the so-called 'instruments of unity'.

---

4 For instance, ACNA Archbishop Foley Beach was invited to the Primates' Meeting in January 2016.

5 On the 'disciplinary measures' applied to TEC, see (particularly point 7): http://www.primates2016.org/articles/2016/01/14/statement-primates-2016. On the decision not to call a Lambeth Conference in 2018, see: http://www.anglicannews.org/news/2014/10/abp-welby-next-lambeth-conference-a-decision-for-the-primates.aspx.

As a picture both of fragility and strength, impressive in terms of its interconnected structure and reach, the spider web is possibly a fitting image for the Anglican Communion. It is beautiful and has a proven track record when facing the winds of change. Nevertheless, as history writes the opening chapters of the twenty-first century, with tensions intensifying over issues concerning human sexuality, the threads are straining, and in places the Anglican web needs mending.

Questions for individual or group reflection

1 What was the most surprising thing that this chapter highlighted for you?
2 What is your own experience of the Anglican Communion? Who do you know who has been on overseas trips to Anglican Churches in other countries, and what sort of things did they do?
3 What is the role of the Archbishop of Canterbury within the Anglican Communion?
4 In what way did the Chicago-Lambeth Quadrilateral boost the significance of bishops for the Anglican Communion?
5 What are the so-called 'instruments of unity' of the Anglican Communion?

PART 2

Essential Sources

The Apostles' Creed

I believe in God, the Father almighty,
creator of heaven and earth.

I believe in Jesus Christ, his only Son, our Lord.
He was conceived by the power of the Holy Spirit
and born of the Virgin Mary.

He suffered under Pontius Pilate,
was crucified, died, and was buried.

He descended to the dead.
On the third day he rose again.
He ascended into heaven,
and is seated at the right hand of the Father.
He will come again to judge the living and the dead.

I believe in the Holy Spirit,
the holy catholic Church,
the communion of saints,
the forgiveness of sins,
the resurrection of the body,
and the life everlasting.

Amen.

The Nicene Creed

We believe in one God,
the Father, the Almighty,
maker of heaven and earth,
of all that is,
seen and unseen.

We believe in one Lord, Jesus Christ,
the only Son of God,
eternally begotten of the Father,
God from God, Light from Light,
true God from true God,
begotten, not made,
of one Being with the Father;
through him all things were made.
For us and for our salvation he came down from heaven,
was incarnate from the Holy Spirit and the Virgin Mary
and was made man.

For our sake he was crucified under Pontius Pilate;
he suffered death and was buried.
On the third day he rose again
in accordance with the Scriptures;
he ascended into heaven
and is seated at the right hand of the Father.
He will come again in glory to judge the living and the dead,
and his kingdom will have no end.

We believe in the Holy Spirit,
the Lord, the giver of life,

who proceeds from the Father and the Son,
who with the Father and the Son is worshipped and glorified,
who has spoken through the prophets.
We believe in one holy catholic and apostolic Church.
We acknowledge one baptism for the forgiveness of sins.
We look for the resurrection of the dead,
and the life of the world to come.

Amen.

The 39 Articles of Religion

1 Of Faith in the Holy Trinity

There is but one living and true God, everlasting, without body, parts, or passions; of infinite power, wisdom, and goodness; the Maker, and Preserver of all things both visible and invisible. And in unity of this Godhead there be three Persons, of one substance, power, and eternity; the Father, the Son, and the Holy Ghost.

2 Of the Word or Son of God, which was made very Man

The Son, which is the Word of the Father, begotten from everlasting of the Father, the very and eternal God, and of one substance with the Father, took Man's nature in the womb of the blessed Virgin, of her substance: so that two whole and perfect Natures, that is to say, the Godhead and Manhood, were joined together in one Person, never to be divided, whereof is one Christ, very God, and very Man; who truly suffered, was crucified, dead, and buried, to reconcile his Father to us, and to be a sacrifice, not only for original guilt, but also for actual sins of men.

3 Of the going down of Christ into Hell

As Christ died for us, and was buried, so also is it to be believed, that he went down into Hell.

4 Of the Resurrection of Christ

Christ did truly rise again from death, and took again his body, with flesh, bones, and all things appertaining to the perfection of Man's nature; wherewith he ascended into Heaven, and there sitteth, until he return to judge all Men at the last day.

5 Of the Holy Ghost

The Holy Ghost, proceeding from the Father and the Son, is of one substance, majesty, and glory, with the Father and the Son, very and eternal God.

6 Of the Sufficiency of the Holy Scriptures for Salvation

Holy Scripture containeth all things necessary to salvation: so that whatsoever is not read therein, nor may be proved thereby, is not to be required of any man, that it should be believed as an article of the Faith, or be thought requisite or necessary to salvation. In the name of the Holy Scripture we do understand those canonical Books of the Old and New Testament, of whose authority was never any doubt in the Church.

Of the Names and Number of the Canonical Books
Genesis Exodus Leviticus Numbers Deuteronomy Joshua Judges Ruth The First Book of Samuel The Second Book of Samuel The First Book of Kings The Second Book of Kings The First Book of Chronicles The Second Book of Chronicles The First Book of Esdras The Second Book of Esdras The Book of Esther The Book of Job The Psalms The Proverbs Ecclesiastes or Preacher Cantica, or Songs of Solomon Four Prophets the greater Twelve Prophets the less.

And the other Books (as Hierome saith) the Church doth read for example of life and instruction of manners; but yet doth it not apply them to establish any doctrine; such are these following:

The Third Book of Esdras The Fourth Book of Esdras The Book of Tobias The Book of Judith The rest of the Book of Esther The Book of Wisdom Jesus the Son of Sirach Baruch the Prophet The Song of the Three Children The Story of Susanna Of Bel and the Dragon The Prayer of Manasses The First Book of Maccabees The Second Book of Maccabees

All the Books of the New Testament, as they are commonly received, we do receive, and account them Canonical.

7 Of the Old Testament

The Old Testament is not contrary to the New: for both in the Old and New Testament everlasting life is offered to Mankind by Christ, who is the only Mediator between God and Man, being both God and Man. Wherefore they are not to be heard, which feign that the old Fathers did look only for transitory promises. Although the Law given from God by Moses, as touching Ceremonies and Rites, do not bind Christian men, nor the Civil precepts thereof ought of necessity to be received in any commonwealth; yet notwithstanding, no Christian man whatsoever is free from the obedience of the Commandments which are called Moral.

8 Of the Creeds

The Three Creeds, Nicene Creed, Athanasius' Creed, and that which is commonly called the Apostles' Creed, ought thoroughly to be received and believed: for they may be proved by most certain warrants of Holy Scripture.

9 Of Original or Birth-Sin

Original sin standeth not in the following of Adam, (as the Pelagians do vainly talk;) but it is the fault and corruption of the

Nature of every man, that naturally is engendered of the off-spring of Adam; whereby man is very far gone from original righteousness, and is of his own nature inclined to evil, so that the flesh lusteth always contrary to the Spirit; and therefore in every person born into this world, it deserveth God's wrath and damnation. And this infection of nature doth remain, yea in them that are regenerated; whereby the lust of the flesh, called in Greek (which some do expound the wisdom, some sensuality, some the affection, some the desire, of the flesh), is not subject to the Law of God. And although there is no condemnation for them that believe and are baptized; yet the Apostle doth confess, that concupiscence and lust hath of itself the nature of sin.

10 Of Free-Will

The condition of Man after the fall of Adam is such, that he cannot turn and prepare himself, by his own natural strength and good works, to faith; and calling upon God. Wherefore we have no power to do good works pleasant and acceptable to God, without the grace of God by Christ preventing us, that we may have a good will, and working with us, when we have that good will.

11 Of the Justification of Man

We are accounted righteous before God, only for the merit of our Lord and Saviour Jesus Christ by Faith, and not for our own works or deservings. Wherefore, that we are justified by Faith only, is a most wholesome Doctrine, and very full of comfort, as more largely is expressed in the Homily of Justification.

12 Of Good Works

Albeit that Good Works, which are the fruits of Faith, and follow after Justification, cannot put away our sins, and endure the severity of God's judgment; yet are they pleasing and acceptable to God in Christ, and do spring out necessarily of a true and lively Faith insomuch that by them a lively Faith may be as evidently known as a tree discerned by the fruit.

13 Of Works before Justification

Works done before the grace of Christ, and the Inspiration of his Spirit, are not pleasant to God, forasmuch as they spring not of faith in Jesus Christ; neither do they make men meet to receive grace, or (as the School-authors say) deserve grace of congruity: yea rather, for that they are not done as God hath willed and commanded them to be done, we doubt not but they have the nature of sin.

14 Of Works of Supererogation

Voluntary Works besides, over and above, God's Command-ments, which they call Works of Supererogation, cannot be taught without arrogancy and impiety: for by them men do declare, that they do not only render unto God as much as they are bound to do, but that they do more for his sake, than of bounden duty is required: whereas Christ saith plainly When ye have done all that are commanded to you, say, We are unprofitable servants.

15 Of Christ alone without Sin

Christ in the truth of our nature was made like unto us in all things, sin only except, from which he was clearly void, both in his flesh, and in his spirit. He came to be the Lamb without spot, who, by sacrifice of himself once made, should take away the sins of the world; and sin (as Saint John saith) was not in him. But all we the rest, although baptized and born again in Christ, yet offend in many things; and if we say we have no sin, we deceive ourselves, and the truth is not in us.

16 Of Sin after Baptism

Not every deadly sin willingly committed after Baptism is sin against the Holy Ghost, and unpardonable. Wherefore the grant of repentance is not to be denied to such as fall into sin after Baptism. After we have received the Holy Ghost, we may depart from grace given, and fall into sin, and by the grace of God we may arise again, and amend our lives. And therefore they are to be condemned, which say, they can no more sin as long as they live here, or deny the place of forgiveness to such as truly repent.

17 Of Predestination and Election

Predestination to Life is the everlasting purpose of God, whereby (before the foundations of the world were laid) he hath constantly decreed by his counsel secret to us, to deliver from curse and damnation those whom he hath chosen in Christ out of mankind, and to bring them by Christ to everlasting salvation, as vessels made to honour. Wherefore, they which be endued with so excellent a benefit of God, be called according to God's purpose by his Spirit working in due season: they through Grace obey the calling: they be justified freely: they be made sons of God by adoption: they be made like the image of his only-begotten Son Jesus Christ: they walk religiously in good works, and at length, by God's mercy, they attain to everlasting felicity.

As the godly consideration of Predestination, and our Election in Christ, is full of sweet, pleasant, and unspeakable comfort to godly persons, and such as feel in themselves the working of the Spirit of Christ, mortifying the works of the flesh, and their earthly members, and drawing up their mind to high and heavenly things, as well because it doth greatly establish and confirm their faith of eternal Salvation to be enjoyed through Christ as because it doth fervently kindle their love towards God: So, for curious and carnal persons, lacking the Spirit of Christ, to have continually before their eyes the sentence of God's Predestination, is a most dangerous downfall, whereby the Devil doth thrust them either into desperation, or into wretchlessness of most unclean living, no less perilous than desperation. Furthermore, we must receive God's promises in such wise, as they be generally set forth to us in Holy Scripture: and, in our doings, that Will of God is to be followed, which we have expressly declared unto us in the Word of God.

18 Of obtaining eternal Salvation only by the Name of Christ

They also are to be had accursed that presume to say, That every man shall be saved by the Law or Sect which he professeth, so that he be diligent to frame his life according to that Law, and the light of Nature. For Holy Scripture doth set out unto us only the Name of Jesus Christ, whereby men must be saved.

19 Of the Church

The visible Church of Christ is a congregation of faithful men, in which the pure Word of God is preached, and the Sacraments be duly ministered according to Christ's ordinance, in all those things that of necessity are requisite to the same.

As the Church of Jerusalem, Alexandria, and Antioch, have erred, so also the Church of Rome hath erred, not only in their living and manner of Ceremonies, but also in matters of Faith.

20 Of the Authority of the Church

The Church hath power to decree Rites or Ceremonies, and authority in Controversies of Faith: and yet it is not lawful for the Church to ordain any thing that is contrary to God's Word written, neither may it so expound one place of Scripture, that it be repugnant to another. Wherefore, although the Church be a witness and a keeper of Holy Writ, yet, as it ought not to decree any thing against the same, so besides the same ought it not to enforce any thing to be believed for necessity of Salvation.

21 Of the Authority of General Councils

General Councils may not be gathered together without the commandment and will of Princes. And when they be gathered together, (forasmuch as they be an assembly of men, whereof all be not governed with the Spirit and Word of God), they may err, and sometimes have erred, even in things pertaining unto God. Wherefore things ordained by them as necessary to salvation have neither strength nor authority, unless it may be declared that they be taken out of holy Scripture.

22 Of Purgatory

The Romish Doctrine concerning Purgatory, Pardons, Worshipping and Adoration, as well of Images as of Relics, and also Invocation of Saints, is a fond thing, vainly invented, and grounded upon no warranty of Scripture, but rather repugnant to the Word of God.

23 Of Ministering in the Congregation

It is not lawful for any man to take upon him the office of public preaching, or ministering the Sacraments in the Congregation, before he be lawfully called, and sent to execute the same. And those we ought to judge lawfully called and sent, which be chosen and called to this work by men who have public authority given unto them in the Congregation, to call and send Ministers into the Lord's vineyard.

24 Of Speaking in the Congregation in such a Tongue as the people understandeth

It is a thing plainly repugnant to the Word of God, and the custom of the Primitive Church to have public Prayer in the Church, or to minister the Sacraments, in a tongue not understood of the people.

25 Of the Sacraments

Sacraments ordained of Christ be not only badges or tokens of Christian men's profession, but rather they be certain sure witnesses, and effectual signs of grace, and God's good will towards us, by the which he doth work invisibly in us, and doth not only quicken, but also strengthen and confirm our Faith in him.

There are two Sacraments ordained of Christ our Lord in the Gospel, that is to say, Baptism, and the Supper of the Lord.

Those five commonly called Sacraments, that is to say, Confirmation, Penance, Orders, Matrimony, and Extreme Unction, are not to be counted for Sacraments of the Gospel, being such as have grown partly of the corrupt following of the Apostles, partly are states of life allowed in the Scriptures, but yet have not like nature of Sacraments with Baptism, and the Lord's Supper, for that they have not any visible sign or ceremony ordained of God.

The Sacraments were not ordained of Christ to be gazed upon, or to be carried about, but that we should duly use them. And in such only as worthily receive the same, they have a wholesome effect or operation: but they that receive them unworthily, purchase to themselves damnation, as Saint Paul saith.

26 Of the Unworthiness of the Ministers, which hinders not the effect of the Sacraments

Although in the visible Church the evil be ever mingled with the good, and sometimes the evil have chief authority in the Ministration of the Word and Sacraments, yet forasmuch as they do not the same in their own name, but in Christ's, and do minister by his commission and authority, we may use their Ministry, both in hearing the Word of God, and in receiving the Sacraments. Neither is the effect of Christ's ordinance taken away by their wickedness, nor the grace of God's gifts diminished from such as by faith, and rightly, do receive the Sacraments ministered unto them; which be effectual, because of Christ's institution and promise, although they be ministered by evil men. Nevertheless, it appertaineth to the discipline of the Church, that inquiry be made of evil Ministers, and that they be accused by those that have knowledge of their offences; and finally, being found guilty, by just judgment be deposed.

27 Of Baptism

Baptism is not only a sign of profession, and mark of difference, whereby Christian men are discerned from others that be not christened, but it is also a sign of Regeneration or New-Birth, whereby, as by an instrument, they that receive Baptism rightly are grafted into the Church; the promises of the forgiveness of sin, and of our adoption to be the sons of God by the Holy Ghost, are visibly signed and sealed, Faith is confirmed, and Grace increased by virtue of prayer unto God.

The Baptism of young Children is in any wise to be retained in the Church, as most agreeable with the institution of Christ.

28 Of the Lord's Supper

The Supper of the Lord is not only a sign of the love that Christians ought to have among themselves one to another, but rather it is a Sacrament of our Redemption by Christ's death: insomuch that to such as rightly, worthily, and with faith, receive the same, the Bread which we break is a partaking of the Body of Christ; and likewise the Cup of Blessing is a partaking of the Blood of Christ.

Transubstantiation (or the change of the substance of Bread and Wine) in the Supper of the Lord, cannot be proved by Holy Writ; but is repugnant to the plain words of Scripture, overthroweth the nature of a Sacrament, and hath given occasion to many superstitions.

The Body of Christ is given, taken, and eaten, in the Supper, only after an heavenly and spiritual manner. And the mean whereby the Body of Christ is received and eaten in the Supper, is Faith.

The Sacrament of the Lord's Supper was not by Christ's ordinance reserved, carried about, lifted up, or worshipped.

29 Of the Wicked, which eat not the Body of Christ in the use of the Lord's Supper

The Wicked, and such as be void of a lively faith, although they do carnally and visibly press with their teeth (as Saint Augustine saith) the Sacrament of the Body and Blood of Christ; yet in no wise are they partakers of Christ: 'but rather, to their condemnation, do eat and drink the sign or Sacrament of so great a thing'.

30 Of both Kinds

The Cup of the Lord is not to be denied to the Lay-people: for both the parts of the Lord's Sacrament, by Christ's ordinance and commandment, ought to be ministered to all Christian men alike.

31 Of the one Oblation of Christ finished upon the Cross

The Offering of Christ once made is that perfect redemption, propitiation, and satisfaction, for all the sins of the whole world, both original and actual; and there is none other satisfaction for sin, but that alone. Wherefore the sacrifices of Masses, in the which it was commonly said, that the Priest did offer Christ for the quick and the dead, to have remission of pain or guilt, were blasphemous fables, and dangerous deceits.

32 Of the Marriage of Priests

Bishops, Priests, and Deacons, are not commanded by God's Law, either to vow the estate of single life, or to abstain from marriage: therefore it is lawful for them, as for all other Christian men, to marry at their own discretion, as they shall judge the same to serve better to godliness.

33 Of excommunicate Persons, how they are to be avoided

That person which by open denunciation of the Church is rightly cut off from the unity of the Church, and excommunicated, ought to be taken of the whole multitude of the faithful, as an Heathen and Publican, until he be openly reconciled by penance, and received into the Church by a Judge that hath authority thereunto.

34 Of the Traditions of the Church

It is not necessary that Traditions and Ceremonies be in all places one, or utterly like; for at all times they have been divers, and may be changed according to the diversity of countries, times, and men's manners, so that nothing be ordained against God's Word. Whosoever, through his private judgment, willingly and purposely, doth openly break the Traditions and Ceremonies of the Church, which be not repugnant to the Word of God, and be ordained and approved by common authority, ought to be rebuked openly, (that others may fear to do the like,) as he that offendeth against the common order of the Church, and hurteth the authority of the Magistrate, and woundeth the consciences of the weak brethren.

Every particular or national Church hath authority to ordain, change, and abolish, Ceremonies or Rites of the Church ordained only by man's authority, so that all things be done to edifying.

35 Of the Homilies

The Second Book of Homilies, the several titles whereof we have joined under this Article, doth contain a godly and wholesome Doctrine, and necessary for these times, as doth the former Book of Homilies, which were set forth in the time of Edward the Sixth; and therefore we judge them to be read in Churches by the Ministers, diligently and distinctly, that they may be understanded of the people.

Of the Names of the Homilies.

1 Of the right Use of the Church.
2 Against Peril of Idolatry.
3 Of repairing and keeping clean of Churches.
4 Of good Works, first of Fasting.
5 Against Gluttony and Drunkenness.
6 Against Excess of Apparel.
7 Of Prayer.
8 Of the Place and Time of Prayer.
9 That Common Prayers and Sacraments ought to be ministered in a known tongue.
10 Of the reverent Estimation of God's Word.
11 Of Alms-doing.
12 Of the Nativity of Christ.
13 Of the Passion of Christ.
14 Of the Resurrection of Christ.
15 Of the worthy receiving of the Sacrament of the Body and Blood of Christ.
16 Of the Gifts of the Holy Ghost.
17 For the Rogation-days.
18 Of the State of Matrimony.
19 Of Repentance.
20 Against Idleness.
21 Against Rebellion.

36 Of Consecration of Bishops and Ministers

The Book of Consecration of Archbishops and Bishops, and Ordering of Priests and Deacons, lately set forth in the time of Edward the Sixth, and confirmed at the same time by authority of Parliament, doth contain all things necessary to such Consecration and Ordering: neither hath it any thing, that of itself is superstitious and ungodly. And therefore whosoever are consecrated or ordered according to the Rites of that Book, since the second year of the forenamed King Edward unto this time, or hereafter shall be consecrated or ordered according to the same Rites; we decree all such to be rightly, orderly, and lawfully consecrated and ordered.

37 Of the Power of the Civil Magistrates

The King's Majesty hath the chief power in this Realm of England, and other his Dominions, unto whom the chief Government of all Estates of this Realm, whether they be Ecclesiastical or Civil, in all causes doth appertain, and is not, nor ought to be, subject to any foreign Jurisdiction.

Where we attribute to the King's Majesty the chief government, by which Titles we understand the minds of some slanderous folks to be offended; we give not our Princes the ministering either of God's Word, or of the Sacraments, the which thing the Injunctions also lately set forth by Elizabeth our Queen do most plainly testify; but that only prerogative, which we see to have been given always to all godly Princes in holy Scriptures by God himself; that is, that they should rule all estates and degrees committed to their charge by God, whether they be Ecclesiastical or Temporal, and restrain with the civil sword the stubborn and evil-doers.

The Bishop of Rome hath no jurisdiction in this Realm of England.

The Laws of the Realm may punish Christian men with death, for heinous and grievous offences.

It is lawful for Christian men, at the commandment of the Magistrate, to wear weapons, and serve in the wars.

38 Of Christian Men's Goods, which are not common

The Riches and Goods of Christians are not common, as touching the right, title, and possession of the same; as certain Anabaptists do falsely boast. Notwithstanding, every man ought, of such things as he possesseth, liberally to give alms to the poor, according to his ability.

39 Of a Christian Man's Oath

As we confess that vain and rash swearing is forbidden Christian men by our Lord Jesus Christ, and James his Apostle, so we judge, that Christian Religion doth not prohibit, but that a man may swear when the Magistrate requireth, in a cause of faith and charity, so it be done according to the Prophet's teaching in justice, judgment, and truth.

Glossary of Anglican terms

Acolyte – a lay person who gives practical assistance to a priest in a church service.

ACNA – Anglican Church in North America, a theologically conservative group of North American Anglicans which divided from The Episcopal Church (TEC) over the issue of homosexuality and the Church.

Adiaphora – a term used in the Reformation to refer to matters of secondary importance over which Anglicans can legitimately agree to disagree.

Affirming Catholicism – a movement within Anglicanism supporting the 'full inclusion' of homosexual Christians in the Church.

Anglican – a term traceable to the Magna Carta meaning the English Church. During the Reformation, it was used to indicate the Church of England over against the Roman Catholic Church. In more recent times, the term denotes a particular expression of Christianity developed in England and then globally.

Anglican Communion – the global family of Anglican Churches present in 165 nations.

Anglican Consultative Council – an advisory body presided over by the Archbishop of Canterbury, whose aim is to help the Anglican Communion realize its objectives as determined in the Lambeth Conference.

Anglican ethos – the notion that – rooted in Scripture, tradition and reason – Anglicanism is a broad and diverse expression of Christianity known for its openness and tolerance on matters that are not 'first order' or essential.

Anglo-Catholicism – a traditional and historically conservative form of Anglicanism with an emphasis on a Catholic spirituality.

ARCIC (Anglican–Roman Catholic International Commission) – a bilateral dialogue aimed at strengthening relations/partnerships between Roman Catholicism and Anglicanism.

Benedictine – relating to the religious order established by St Benedict and/or to practices outlined in the rule of St Benedict.

Book of Common Prayer (BCP) – the traditional liturgy of the Church of England, published in a handful of authorized versions since the mid-sixteenth century; also, the official Anglican liturgy of other Anglican Provinces.

Canon law – the laws that govern a Church, its internal structures, and those who exercise roles of responsibility within it.

Catechesis/catechism – an ancient practice of learning key doctrinal truths (a catechism) of Christianity by a repetitive question and answer method.

Celtic Christianity – a form of spirituality that draws on the wisdom/writings of the 'Celtic fathers and mothers' – that is, the British saints in the first few centuries of the Church.

Charismatic movement – a renewal movement with a focus on the fruit and gifts of the Holy Spirit, whose roots can be traced to the Church of England in the 1950s and 1960s.

CMS – Church Mission Society, the world's largest Anglican mission agency whose roots can be traced to the evangelical movement in eighteenth-century England.

Common Worship (CW) – the latest liturgical series used in the Church of England alongside the Book of Common Prayer.

Comprehensiveness – a term that refers to the Anglican ethos of encouraging diversity on a range of issues while retaining an underlying unity.

Creeds – ancient statements of core Christian beliefs such as the Apostles' Creed and the Nicene Creed.

Crucifer – the person who carries the cross in the procession in a church service.

Daily Offices – the service of Morning and Evening Prayer that clergy in the Church of England are required to pray through either corporately or privately each day.

Daily Prayer App – an 'app' available for free download containing the Church of England's Daily Offices.

Deanery – a geographical area within a diocese consisting of a group of parishes.

Diocese – a geographical region in a Province presided over by a 'diocesan' bishop.

Elizabethan Religious Settlement (the) – the attempt to unite different and opposing religious factions in one moderately reformed Church of England, set out in two Acts of Parliament: the Act of Supremacy (1558) – which confirmed Elizabeth I as 'supreme governor' of the Church – and the Act of Uniformity (1559) – which standardized the Book of Common Prayer.

Episcopal/episcopal – 'Episcopal' is an alternative name to 'Anglican', used, for example, in the Church in Scotland and the USA. The word 'episcopal' derives from the Greek for 'overseer' or 'bishop'.

Episcopacy – governance by bishops or the specific term of office of a bishop.

Episcopate – the order of bishops.

Eucharist – from the Greek 'thanksgiving', this is another way of referring to Holy Communion.

GAFCON (Global Anglican Future Conference) – a conservative movement within Anglicanism concerned to maintain an orthodox stance on issues relating to human sexuality.

Historic formularies (the) – the 39 Articles of Religion, the Book of Common Prayer and the Ordering of Bishops, Priests and Deacons as expressed in the Ordinal.

Ignatian spirituality – a form of spirituality that draws on the writings/spiritual disciplines of St Ignatius of Loyola.

Instruments of unity/instruments of the Communion – four interlinked 'instruments' to manage and promote the Anglican Communion: the Archbishop of Canterbury, the Anglican Consultative Council, the Primates' Meeting and the Lambeth Conference.

Lambeth Conference – normally held every ten years, this is the gathering of bishops from the Anglican Communion; it is held in Canterbury and convened by the Archbishop of Canterbury.

Lambeth Quadrilateral (Chigago-Lambeth Quadrilateral) – the four founding/guiding principles of the Anglican Communion, namely, the Holy Scriptures, the Creeds (Apostles' and Nicene), the sacraments of Holy Communion and Holy Baptism and the historic episcopate.

Lectio divina – a Benedictine form of meditation on a passage or verse of Scripture that combines reading, prayer and contemplation.

Lectionary – the Anglican cycle of set Bible readings for Sundays and weekdays.

Lex orandi lex credendi – the principle that the words spoken/prayed in Anglican worship express Anglican (doctrinal) belief.

Litany – a series of intercessory prayers/petitions, sometimes inviting responses from the congregation.

Liturgy – the order for worship in a church service and/or the words/prayers/actions that comprise a service of worship.

LLM – Licensed Lay Minister, formerly referred to as Lay Readers, these are trained lay ministers who exercise a pastoral/teaching ministry alongside clergy.

Lord's Table – the name given to the table where Holy Communion is celebrated; it is also referred to as 'altar' in more Catholic church traditions.

Ordinal – the authorized liturgy for the ordination of bishops, priests and deacons.

Parish – the local geographical region served by a parish priest and his/her team.

PCC (Parochial Church Council) – consisting of clergy and laity, it is the legal body responsible for the management of a parish church.

Primates – archbishops who preside over an Anglican Province.

Primates' Meeting – an advisory body of archbishops presided over by the Archbishop of Canterbury.

Province – a large national or transnational region presided over by an archbishop or 'primate'; there are 39 in the Anglican Communion.

Sacraments – classically defined as 'outward signs of internal graces', Anglicanism recognizes Holy Communion and Holy Baptism as 'the sacraments' since these were instituted by Jesus himself.

Synod – an assembly of clergy and laity of a particular region, be that local (e.g. deanery), regional (e.g. diocesan) or national (i.e. in the Church of England, the General Synod; known in TEC as 'General Convention').

The Episcopal Church (TEC) – formally ECUSA, the Province of the Anglican Communion based in the USA but also covering some Central/Southern American Anglican churches.

The 39 Articles of Religion – a compendium of Anglican doctrinal principles/church practices drawn up in the English Reformation.

Via media – a Latin phrase that refers to Anglicanism as a 'middle way' between Roman Catholicism on the one hand, and more Reformed expressions of Protestantism on the other.

Bibliography

Chapter 1

Avis, Paul, *Anglicanism and the Christian Church*, London: T&T Clark, 2002.

Chapman, Mark D., Clarke, Sathianathan and Percy, Martyn (eds), *The Oxford Handbook of Anglican Studies*, Oxford: Oxford University Press, 2016.

Edwards, David L., *What Anglicans Believe in the Twenty-first Century*, London: Continuum, 2002.

Goodhew, David (ed.), *Growth and Decline in the Anglican Communion: 1980 to the Present*, London: Routledge, 2017.

Heywood, David, *Reimagining Ministry*, London: SCM Press, 2011.

Jenkins, Philip, *The Next Christendom: The Coming of Global Christianity*, Oxford: Oxford University Press, 2002.

Lings, George, 'Chapter 9¾: Can the Idea of a Reproductive Strand in Church Identity Fit with Church of England Ecclesiology?', Church Army website http://churcharmy.org.

Percy, Martyn, *Anglicanism: Confidence, Commitment and Communion*, Farnham: Ashgate, 2013.

Podmore, Colin, *Aspects of Anglican Identity*, London: Church House Publishing, 2005.

Ross, Cathy and Walls, Andrew, *Mission in the 21st Century: Exploring the Five Marks of Global Mission*, Maryknoll, NY: Orbis, 2008.

Spencer, Nick, *Doing Good: A Future for Christianity in the 21st Century*, London: Theos, 2017.

Sykes, S. W., *The Integrity of Anglicanism*, London: Mowbray, 1978.

Chapter 2

Chapman, Mark, D., Clarke, Sathianathan and Percy, Martyn (eds), *The Oxford Handbook of Anglican Studies*, Oxford: Oxford University Press, 2016.

Heinze, Rudolph W., *Reform and Conflict: From the Medieval World to the Wars of Religion* AD *1350–1648, Volume Four*, Oxford: Monarch Books, 2006.

Kings, Graham, 'Canal, River and Rapids: Contemporary Evangelicalism in the Church of England', *Anvil*, 20.3, 2003, pp. 167–84.

Chapter 3

Common Worship: Daily Prayer, London: Church House Publishing, 2005.

Kennedy, David, *Using Common Worship: Times and Seasons*, London: Church House Publishing, 2006.

Walton, Izaak, *The Compleat Angler*, New York: Modern Library, 1939.

Chapter 4

Avis, Paul, *Anglicanism and the Christian Church*, London: T&T Clark, 2002.

Beach, Mark, *Using Common Worship Holy Communion: A Practical Guide to the New Services*, London: Church House Publishing, 2000.

Croft, Steven, *Ministry in Three Dimensions*, London: Darton, Longman and Todd, 1999.

Hooker, Richard, *Laws of Ecclesiastical Polity*, Book V, Oxford: Clarendon Press, 1876.

Jewel, John, *The Apology of the Church of England*, London: Cassell and Company, 1888.

Meyer, Carl, S., *Cranmer's Selected Writings*, London: SPCK, 1961.

Chapter 5

Atherstone, A. and Goddard, A., *Good Disagreement? Grace and Truth in a Divided Church*, London: Lion, 2015.

Bradshaw, Timothy (ed.), *The Way Forward? Christian Voices on Homosexuality and the Church*, London: SCM Press, 2003.

Brown, Malcolm (ed.), *Anglican Social Theology*, London: Church House Publishing, 2014.

Chapman, Mark, *Anglican Theology*, London: T&T Clark, 2012.

Harris, Harriet and Shaw, Jane (eds), *The Call for Women Bishops*, London: SPCK, 2004.

Linzey, Andrew and Kirker, Richard (eds), *Gays and the Future of Anglicanism: Responses to the Windsor Report*, Winchester: O Books, 2005.

Percy, Martyn, *Anglicanism: Confidence, Commitment and Communion*, Farnham: Ashgate, 2013.

Percy, Martyn, *The Future Shapes of Anglicanism: Currents, Contours, Charts*, London: Routledge, 2017.

Chapter 6

Bonhoeffer, Dietrich, *The Cost of Discipleship*, London: SCM Press, 1996.

Hope, Susan, *Mission-shaped Spirituality*, London: Church House Publishing, 2006.

Rowling, Cathy and Gooder, Paula, *Reader Ministry Explored*, London: SPCK, 2009.

Tanner, Mark, *The PCC Member's Essential Guide*, London: Church House Publishing, 2015.

Chapter 7

Bunting, Ian (ed.), *Celebrating the Anglican Way*, London: Grove Books, 1996.

Markham, Ian, Terry, Justyn and Steffensen, Leslie Nunez, *The Wiley-Blackwell Companion to the Anglican Communion*, Oxford: Blackwell, 2013.

McGrath, Alister E., *The Renewal of Anglicanism*, London: SPCK, 1993.

Throup, Marcus, 'Learning to Be: A Brazilian Case Study in Social Injustice', *Common Ground Journal*, 3.2, 2006, pp. 33–45.

Walker, David, *God's Belongers*, Abingdon: Bible Reading Fellowship, 2017.

Wells, Samuel, *What Anglicans Believe*, Norwich: Canterbury Press, 2011.

Wright, N. T., *The New Testament and the People of God*, London: SPCK, 1992.

Wright, Tom, *Simply Christian*, London: SPCK, 2006.

Chapter 8

Chapman, Mark, *Anglicanism: A Very Short Introduction*, Oxford: Oxford University Press, 2006.

Chapman, Mark D., Clarke, Sathianathan and Percy, Martyn (eds), *The Oxford Handbook of Anglican Studies*, Oxford: Oxford University Press, 2016.

Markham, Ian, Terry, Justyn and Steffensen, Leslie Nunez (eds), *The Wiley-Blackwell Companion to the Anglican Communion*, Oxford: Blackwell, 2013.

Wells, Samuel, *What Anglicans Believe*, Norwich: Canterbury Press, 2011.